SOCIAL CHANGE IN THE FAMILY

SOCIAL CHANGE IN THE FAMILY

Jan Dizard

COMMUNITY AND FAMILY STUDY CENTER
UNIVERSITY OF CHICAGO

COMMUNITY AND FAMILY STUDY CENTER
UNIVERSITY OF CHICAGO

BOOKS AND MONOGRAPHS

Ernest W. Burgess and Donald J. Bogue, editors
Contributions to Urban Sociology

Donald J. Bogue
Skid Row in American Cities

Henry S. Shryock, Jr.
Population Mobility within the United States

Donald J. Bogue, editor
Sociological Contributions to Family Planning Research

Donald J. Bogue, editor
Motivation and Communication for Family Planning: Selections from Lectures and Reports of Four Summer Workshops

Jan Dizard
Social Change in the Family

Printed in the United States of America

PREFACE

That longitudinal studies are essential in order to study social change with precision is a principle that is frequently declared, but seldom acted upon. As he did in so many other cases, Ernest W. Burgess was among the first to recognize this principle--and to act upon it. The present monograph brings to fruition his dream of studying longitudinally a sample of married couples after fifteen years of conjugal life. In 1954 he had begun a third round of interviews to follow up once again the sample of couples who had been respondents in the 1939 Burgess-Wallin panel reported in their Engagement and Marriage. Because the couples were widely scattered, the task proved to be tedius and time consuming; years were consumed in data collection. Age, failing health, and full-time interest in the field of sociology of aging which he had meanwhile helped to found and develop combined to keep Burgess from exploiting these materials. An outstanding but partial analysis was made by Dr. Peter C. Pineo in his doctoral dissertation, Dyadic and Change Analysis of Marriage and Divorce (University of Chicago, 1960). One of the obligations which this writer inherited when the Community and Family Study Center was reorganized in 1961 was sponsorship of the preparation of a comprehensive final report based on this third wave of interviewing.

Mr. Jan Dizard, an outstanding graduate student who had a fundamental interest in the study of the family, was offered these data to tabulate and analyze, with financial and technical assistance from the Center. This he undertook to do with skill and enthusiasm. Professor Burgess was still in reasonably good health at the time and took a very active interest in the project. He gave guidance and answered questions as they arose. As Professor Burgess' health declined, Mr. Dizard not only assumed more responsibility for the work but helped attend to his personal needs. Dizard is the last of a long line of distinguished scholars who began as Dr. Burgess' research acolyte and ended as his collaborator. Because the plan of analysis and the manuscript is completely that of Dr. Dizard, despite his protest I have asked him to be listed as sole author of this report.

The present work is a revised version of Mr. Dizard's doctoral dissertation. It was planned and conducted with the intent that it be a summary analysis of the third round of interviewing. The reader will find it provocative and suggestive of many ideas for continued research. Let us hope that it helps bring more action in the form of longitudinal studies in the future.

Donald J. Bogue
October, 1968

AUTHOR'S PREFACE

With the onset of the industrial revolution came pressures to wrest control of placement in the occupational structure from the hands of kinship based ascriptive processes in order to free individuals to seek their own levels in the emerging industrial order. The transition was not easy, nor was it smooth. Among many dislocations, the one that will concern us in this work will be the disruption of family roles attendant on the industrial revolution. The dilemma was that behavior required to maintain the integrity of the family diverged from the kinds of behavior necessary to keep the wheels of industry in motion. The response to this dilemma, in the short run erratic and gruding, was, in the long run, to attempt to segregate the two activities, familial and occupational, as much as possible. Gradually, occupational roles became the province of men; women were discouraged from working and sustaining a meaningful role in the economy and only the threat of poverty was sufficient excuse for the wife to leave the home to seek employment.

By focusing on this solution to the dilemma, it soon became, in the literature of sociology, *the* solution to the contradiction between occupation and family. The present study, though limited in time and representativeness, indicates that this solution may be imperfect and that it is not wise to close accounts on this contradiction for it has left women in what may amount to an untenable position: removed from the occupational structure, she is expected to understand and abide by her husband's occupationally conditioned *raison d'etre*. This study analyzes some of the implications of this situation as they manifest themselves in the course of four hundred marriages.

In the quarter-century spanned by this study, many individuals lended their talents and energies and were it not for them, my work, begun in 1963, would have been impossible. Unfortunately, as this study was begun shortly before my birth, most of the contributors to this study remain anonymous to me. I would like to record here my gratitude to all these unknown contributors. Financial support for this study has come from several sources. The initial funding was by the National Institute of Health. Support for this specific project was generously provided by the Social Science Research Committee and the Community and Family Study Center, both of the University of Chicago. The Community and Family Study Center gave of much more than money. It provided me with a congenial and stimulating environment, without which I fear my progress would have been slight. Donald J. Bogue, Morris Janowitz, David Street and Richard Flacks read all or parts of earlier versions of this manuscript and their comments and criticisms were most helpful. My greatest debt is to Ernest W. Burgess. Not only did he allow me to use the data he so painstakingly and foresightedly had collected over a period of fifteen years, he also gave freely of his time to discuss the manuscript and the ideas contained in it. Whatever is of value in this study can be traced to these discussions. Needless to say, the shortcomings of this study are to be laid at my doorstep. Finally, I would like to thank my wife, Robin, and my son, Jesse. Were it not for them, the results of this study would have left me with a dim view of marriage.

TABLE OF CONTENTS

I

INTRODUCTION

In 1939, Ernest W. Burgess, collaborating with Paul Wallin, began a study designed to test and refine the observations made in Burgess' and Cottrell's earlier study of the factors associated with "success and failure in marriage."[1] The 1939 study was initially conceived of in terms of a two-wave longitudinal study in which couples were to be asked to fill out questionnaires during their engagement and again after having been married for several years. Burgess and Wallin hoped to predict from the engagement inventories of the husbands and wives-to-be to the marital adjustment and happiness of the husbands and wives after marriage, using the subsequent marriage data as a check on the accuracy of prediction. While much valuable information was obtained from this ambitious research program, Burgess and Wallin were forced to conclude that their predictions, based on a highly detailed line of questioning, were slightly (if at all) better than chance. Taking all predictive items together, only approximately 25 percent of the observed post-marriage variance in husband-wife adjustment scores was accounted for.[2] Burgess and Wallin gave four possible reasons for this failure:[3]

1. The premarital inventories were inadequate.
2. The postmarital measures of success were unsatisfactory.
3. Unforseen conditions had appeared after marriage that could not have been taken into account during engagement.
4. Husbands and wives differ in ability to adjust to one another and to changing circumstances and this ability was not allowed for.

While Burgess and Wallin were not insensitive to the difficulties and shortcomings that inhere in any effort to measure such phenomena as marital success, they felt that the principle substantive oversight in their study was the failure to take into adequate account the dynamic element resulting both from changes in the social circumstances in which the couple finds itself and changes in the relationship between individual husbands and wives. In the nature of things, Burgess and Wallin were forced to speculate about both of these sources of dynamic. But, thirteen years after the second wave, a third questionnaire was mailed out to the couples in an effort to collect additional data that would help in an analysis of the changes in the husband-wife relationship that made prediction based on engagement data problematic. The central concern of the present investigation is to examine the changes that take place in marriage. Specifically, the following question will be asked: In what ways, and for what reasons, does the husband-wife relationship change over time?[4] In order to begin to address this question, we need first to examine in some detail the nature of the husband-wife relationship as it existed in the early years of marriage. Before doing this, however, a few words regarding the time span involved in this study and the sample to be analyzed seem in order.

As indicated above, the study was begun in 1939. At that time, Burgess and Wallin solicited engaged couples for the study by asking Burgess' students at the University of Chicago to ask any engaged couples they knew of to take part in the study. One thousand engaged couples were recruited in this manner and questionnaires were administered separately to both the men and women involved. The sample, as we shall see, was not even remotely a cross-section of the population and, obviously, was not random. Three years later (1942), these couples were again given questionnaires to fill out. Because of the disruption of the war, this second phase of the study lasted until 1946 and netted 666 couples, couples who had been married from 1 to 6 years. The second phase, the "early marriage" phase, shall be the starting point for our analysis. In 1955, the third wave was begun and by 1960, 400 couples had responded. This group of 400 couples will be our subject matter.[5] Let us now examine some of the more important characteristics of these 400 couples as they were reported in the early marriage phase of the study.

The husbands and wives in our sample are, by and large, of middle class origins. Without going into great detail--a comprehensive description of the social origins of the sample is given by Burgess and Wallin[6]--Table 1-1 summarizes the occupational and religious background of the sample. As is clear from this table, husbands and wives are predominantly urban (few parents were farmers) and typically had white collar status, many being the sons or daughters of relatively high status parents--professionals, managers and the like. All are white and native born; the majority are Protestants; Jews are over represented while Roman Catholics are under represented. Religious intermarriage, while existent, is not common--only 13 percent of the couples are religiously heterogeneous, the most frequent combination being Protestant-Jewish intermarriage. Cross-

Table 1-1.--OCCUPATIONAL AND RELIGIOUS BACKGROUNDS OF HUSBAND AND WIFE

Background item	Husband	Wife
Total.......	100.0	100.0
Father's occupation		
Professional.....	17.2	15.0
Managerial.......	23.0	32.0
Clerical-sales...	21.2	20.5
Farm............	6.0	3.8
Blue-collar......	22.2	18.5
Retired, no information.......	10.2	10.2
Total.......	100.0	100.0
Religion		
Protestant.......	49.2	53.5
Catholic.........	9.0	8.2
Jew.............	21.8	23.5
None, other......	13.3	9.2
No information...	6.2	5.5

class marriages are also rather infrequent in this group. Comparing husband and wife in terms of each's father's occupation, we find that 12 percent of the marriages involved spouses of widely differing occupational backgrounds. That is, 12 percent of the couples had one spouse with parents two or more occupational steps removed from the parents of the other spouse. In short, this sample of couples is quite homogamous.

Given their backgrounds and the fact that the couples were selected on the basis of their acquaintance with college students, it is not surprising to note that husbands and wives are quite well educated. At the time of the engagement survey, 64 percent of the husbands and 49 percent of the wives had completed at least three years of college.[7] As the educational achievements of husband and wife indicate, these couples were well on their way toward at least continuing the status of their parents.[8] As with most well educated middle class people, these individuals tended to marry in their early

Table 1-2. --EDUCATION, AGE AT MARRIAGE AND ORGANIZATIONAL MEMBERSHIP OF HUSBAND AND WIFE

Indice	Husband	Wife
Education		
High school.......	18.2	32.2
1-3 years college.	24.3	25.8
B.A. degree.......	21.8	27.5
Graduate work.....	34.5	13.2
Age at marriage		
Under 20..........	...	4.5
20-24.............	51.2	72.2
25-29.............	40.2	19.8
30 or over........	8.4	3.3
Organizational memberships		
None..............	33.2	38.5
One...............	28.9	26.5
Two...............	17.4	19.4
Three or more.....	20.5	15.6

and middle twenties, over 90 percent marrying before the age of thirty (see Table 1-2). As is also typical of this stratum of the population, the majority of husbands and wives belonged to at least one professional or community organization (excluding membership in churches). In sum, this particular group of husbands and wives possess remarkably few of those characteristics ordinarily associated with marital discord. They have similar--and advantaged--backgrounds, have achieved relatively high status by the time of marriage and appear to be (or are rapidly becoming) respected members in their communities. And what of their marriages?

Husband and Wife: The Early Years of Marriage

Predictably, most husbands and wives reported quite high levels of marital adjustment in the early years of marriage (see Table 1-3).

Table 1-3.--EARLY MARRIAGE LEVELS OF MARITAL ADJUSTMENT: HUSBAND AND WIFE

Marital adjustment score	Husband	Wife
Total.....	100.0	100.0
Low..........	11.0	8.5
Moderate.....	40.2	36.2
High.........	48.8	55.2

The Marital Adjustment Score (MAS) is the general measure of marital unity developed and refined by Burgess and his associates.[9] A high score on the MAS is indicative of a close, companionate relationship in which husband and wife cooperate, share authority and suffer no basic differences of opinion. A high score, in addition, means that the individual is happy with his (her) choice of spouse and is willing (if not eager) to continue the relationship. In more esoteric language, the MAS measures 1) the extent to which husband and wife have worked out a harmonious role relationship and 2) the extent to which the marital relationship gratifies and sustains the commitment of husband and wife to their marriage.[10] Let us first examine the role relationships that typified the newly formed marriages of our 400 couples.

One of the most difficult tasks facing newlyweds is the building of consensus--agreement on how things are going to be done. How should family finances be handled? How should household tasks be shared (or should they)? What about in-laws? Friends? When should we begin to have children and how many should we have? These and a host of other issues have to be settled in some measure, though not necessarily permanently, if husband and wife are to be able to live together in peace and amity. In order to discover the extent to which each spouse feels that such issues have been settled, Burgess developed what has come to be called the "Consensus Index." In addition to the issues indicated above, the Consensus Index inquires of the extent of agreement on religion, politics and so on.[11] The higher the score, the greater the perceived agreement between spouses. Table 1-4, panel 1, presents the early marriage Consensus scores for husband and wife.

Table 1-4. -- INDICES OF EARLY MARRIAGE ROLE RELATIONSHIPS: HUSBAND AND WIFE

Indices of role relationship	Husband	Wife
Consensus		
Low................	12.8	9.8
Moderate...........	67.0	72.5
High...............	20.2	17.7
Dominance		
Low................	30.2	34.8
Moderate...........	52.8	49.5
High...............	17.0	15.7
Traditionalism		
Low................	31.0	25.8
Moderate...........	51.5	52.2
High...............	17.5	22.0

It is clear that most husbands and wives do not find themselves in complete agreement with one another. Of course, almost no couples operate on the basis of complete unanimity. Short of this, however, it is important to note that very few husbands and wives report frequent disagreements and/or serious quarreling. This, we argue, is probably as significant as finding total agreement, for what this represents is a situation in which husband and wife, in spite of some disagreement, were able to resolve differences without resorting to serious disputes. In other words, it would appear that a reasonably harmonious _modus vivendi_ has been established in the vast majority of cases.

Some insight into the nature of this _modus vivendi_ can be gleaned from a consideration of another important aspect of husband-wife role relationships--_viz._, authority relations between husband and wife. When disagreements arise, as they appear to in most cases, how are they resolved: by give and take, or by one spouse regularly giving in to the other? To ask this question is to essentially enquire of the patterns of dominance in the husband-wife relationship. In order to assess this aspect of the marital relationship, we shall refer to the Dominance-Submission Score that was developed by Burgess. This score is comprised of fifteen questions involving the extent to which the individual husband or wife seeks hegemony in his or her relationship. A high score on this measure of role relationship denotes a spouse who angers easily when failing to get his (her) own way, whose temper is mentioned by his or her spouse as an unsettling aspect of the marriage and who frequently does get his or her own way. A low score indicates the opposite of the above characteristics--i.e., a submissive individual.

In Table 1-4, panel 2, we see that one of the reasons for the absence of serious quarreling noted above, even in the face of a less than perfect agreement between husband and wife, is predominantly attributable to the fact that very few spouses appear either argumentative or domineering. When disagreements do occur, few husbands or wives steadfastly insist on their own way; most report talking things over and reaching decisions by "give and take." In short, authority seems to be relatively equally distributed between husband and wife in most of the couples we are dealing with.

Indeed, most husbands and wives tend to raise egalitarianism between spouses to a principle, for when we examine the amount of "traditionalism" each desires in marriage, we find that very few of our respondents fully accept the traditional models of husband-wife behavior. Specifically, the Traditionalism Index consists of five statements as follows: 1) "The husband should wear the pants"; 2) "the wife should have money of her own"; 3) "children should be held to strict discipline"; 4) "husband and wife should not have had sexual intercourse with each other before marriage"; and 5) "young people should be trained never to indulge in 'petting' or 'spooning'." As is clear from an examination of the distribution of scores on this index (see Table 1-4, panel 3), most husbands and wives do not find themselves in accord with the traditional responses to these statements.[12] By dissenting, they indicate that, for them at least, the family should not be husband dominated and strictly--and puritanically--ruled.

While it is not our intent to fit these couples into a neat typology of styles of role relationship, it seems rather clear that the vast majority of these couples have developed husband-wife role relationships that approximate what has come to be called, in family sociology, a "jointly organized" role relationship.[13] The implications of this label are reasonably clear. As Rainwater puts it:

> In these (jointly organized) relationships, husband and wife undertake many activities...together with a minimum of task differentiation and separation of interest. They not only plan the affairs of the family together but also exchange many household tasks and spend much of their leisure time together.[14]

If we think in terms of spheres of activity, one sphere for each spouse, it appears that in these couples at the early years stage of marriage, the husband's sphere of activities overlaps considerably with the wife's sphere of activities. The consensus they express indicates that there is, for these couples, a rather high degree of agreement on values and behavior and, where there are differences, the lines of communication and decision-making are open and accessible to each spouse equally. And, in addition, husband and wife tend to see this type of a relationship as a central value in marriage, not just a pragmatic adjustment. It is this type of relationship that Burgess has suggested is emerging with full force in modern, industrial society, calling such a marriage a "companionate" relationship.[15] Other researchers have found that this type of role relationship is quite typical of the middle class in our society and, given the thoroughgoing middle class status of our sample, this characteristic seems more than apt for the bulk of our sample.[16]

Numerous observers, Burgess foremost among them, have noted that marriages characterized by joint role organization are heavily dependent upon personal gratification and commitment for continued viability. The _raison d'etre_ of such marriages is that they are mutually satisfying and, lacking many of the former institutional safeguards surrounding marriage, the failure of husband and wife to be happy with marriage significantly undermines the stability of the marital bond.[17] That is, the joint role organization is both dependent on and results in the generation of personal gratification and commitment. In both of these respects, the early marriage reports of husband and wife indicate substantial happiness with and commitment to marriage.

The happiness of husband and wife was measured in the Burgess-Wallin study by providing each spouse with a checklist series of statements of the following type: "Although my mate and I get along well together, I think I could be happier married to someone else," or "I cannot conceive of anyone being more happily married than I am." Sixteen of these statements were presented and each respondent was asked to check those that represented his (her) feelings. Four additional items were included and dealt with the respondent's estimate of continued happiness. High scores indicate that no negative comments were checked and that the respondent believed himself likely to enjoy continued happiness. Low scores indicate some unhappiness at present and a good deal of pessimism with regard to the future. As is clear from Table 1-5, panel 1, most husbands and wives fall somewhere between the extremes of euphoria and unhappiness. As the cumulative evidence shall make clear, however, this moderation in happiness seems to connote not a lack of gratification from or a cynicism toward marriage but, rather, a fairly "realistic" appraisal of their condition. In terms of the questions asked, in other words, our well educated husbands and wives could probably conceive of per-

Table 1-5. --INDICES OF EARLY MARRIAGE GRATIFICATION AND COMMITMENT FOR HUSBANDS AND WIVES

Indices	Husband	Wife
Happiness		
Low	14.0	12.0
Moderate	59.2	51.0
High	26.8	37.0
Idealization*		
Low	14.6	12.6
Moderate	50.2	45.7
High	35.2	41.3
Love		
Somewhat	28.5	17.5
Very much	46.2	42.5
Extraordinarily	25.2	40.0
Permanence		
Low	3.0	5.0
Moderate	18.2	19.5
High	78.8	75.5

*Due to nonresponse, the number of cases for Idealization are decreased: Husband = 398, Wife = 395.

sons being more happily married but this does not mean that the respondent himself is unhappily married; everything points in the opposite direction.

The feeling that one has chosen a spouse well ought to be another indication of a gratifying marriage. We are not interested, here, in whether or not the individual regards his (her) spouse as the "one and only." While this is obviously a strong theme in our culture, we think it sufficient that spouses view one another as positively acceptable though not necessarily the best of all possible mates. To this end, we shall utilize an index called (we think inappropriately) the Idealization Index. This index calls for respondent ratings of the degree to which their spouses are easy to anger, moody, irritable, selfish and stubborn. The higher the score, the less the individual attributes any or all of these characteristics to his or her spouse. As with happiness, we see that few husbands and wives are disillusioned with their selection, more are entirely positive (in terms of the above items at least) toward their spouses, and the majority fall somewhere between these two extremes (see Table 1-5, panel 2). That is, most husbands and wives see each other as people, possessing in slight degree some unbecoming characteristics but not to the extent of causing extreme misgivings on the part of either spouse.

Closely related to the evaluation of one's spouse's good or bad characteristics are the feelings of love felt for each other. It would be a mistake to overestimate the extent to which love and idealization overlap, for there is ample evidence to indicate that love is not entirely blind.[18] In any event, loving and feeling loved no doubt contribute greatly to the extent the marriage pleases the marriage partners. As a measure of love, each respondent was asked to rate the extent of his (her) love for his (her) spouse on a ten point scale, with the extremes of the scale being identified as "extraordinarily in love" and "somewhat in love." Husbands and wives in our sample express no small degree of love for one another (Table 1-5, panel 3). Wives especially are likely to report rather high levels of love for their husbands. This, coupled with the generally optimistic responses in regard to happiness and idealization, indicates a confident and pleasurable regard for one's marriage--while being less than idyllic, it is far from being a misery.

This interpretation is borne out when we consider husband's and wife's evaluations of the durability of their relationship. That is, when asked if they have ever considered separation and/or divorce, husbands and wives overwhelmingly reply in the negative (Table 1-5, panel 4). Specifically, husband and wife were asked: "Have you ever considered separating (divorcing) from your spouse: seriously, somewhat seriously, not seriously, have never considered it." The responses were weighted from four to one (never and seriously, respectively) for both divorce and separation and combined into the Permanence Index. High scores indicate a response of "never" to both separation and divorce. On the basis of the distribution of scores for husband and wife, it becomes clear that the slight moderation in responses to love, idealization and happiness do not represent ambivalence toward marriage--virtually everyone is strongly committed to his own marriage.

This brief investigation of the couples in early marriage has brought out an essentially ideal set of marriages. Typical sources of strain--e.g., religious, economic and educational differences--are by and large nonexistent for these couples. The husband-wife relationship is highly informal and egalitarian; and one in which husband and wife report no serious conflicts with regard to role expectations and performance. For most, gratification is substantial and commitment is very high. Indeed, it is almost as if these husbands and wives had carefully read the Burgess-Wallin study before their marriages. But reading that volume, helpful though it may be for couples planning to get married, gives little hint as to what takes place after the early years of marriage. The remainder of this work will be devoted to analyzing the subsequent changes that took place in these 400 marriages. To this end, we will now turn briefly to a consideration of the sources of change as outlined by Burgess and Wallin, pursuing their formulation further and thereby lay the basis for the analysis that follows.

Burgess and Wallin, although unable to pursue their hunch, saw the sources of dynamism as falling into two categories: those internal to the husband-wife relationship--e.g., differences in the adaptability of husband and wife--and those external to the husband-wife bond--e.g., changes in the milieu within which husband and wife operate. In other words, they did not see the family as a microcosm of society, a self-enclosed unit which can be understood solely in terms of husband-wife relationships. Further, the family was placed in a larger social context, changes in which can produce changes in the family. One of the problems, then, of predicting from engagement to marriage lies in the fact that the act of marriage, itself, puts the two individuals in a new social situation; people react differently to the now married individuals and new things are expected of them. Of course, this process of change continues throughout the life of the couple.

In 1960, Peter C. Pineo, then a student of Burgess', began the analysis of the changes undergone by the 400 couples being dealt with here since the time of early marriage.[19] In so doing, he came to the conclusion that the changes that took place in the husband-wife relationship resulted from "...unforeseen changes in situation, personality or behavior...."[20] Again we find the internal-external line being drawn. Pineo's analysis, however, indicated that personality changes did not seem to have too much bearing on the changes observed in the husband-wife relationship.[21] Pineo did not investigate the influence of external change.

In the analysis that follows, we shall take as our point of departure the detailed investigation of the changes that took place in the internal aspects of the husband-wife relationship and, in addition, we shall analyze the changes in the ways husband and wife related to the external environment. One chapter will be devoted to each area of change. Then, we shall explore the ways in which these two types of change interact with one another, looking specifically at the impact which changes in husband's and wife's relationships to external milieu have on the changes in the husband-wife relationship. In short, we will attempt to specify the "conditions" that Burgess and Wallin felt to be possible sources for dynamic.

FOOTNOTES

1. Ernest W. Burgess and Leonard S. Cottrell, Jr., Predicting Success or Failure in Marriage (New York: Prentice Hall, 1939).

2. Ernest W. Burgess and Paul Wallin, Engagement and Marriage (New York: Lippincott, 1953), p. 620.

3. Ibid.

4. In posing this question, we depart from the initial aim of Burgess and Wallin--viz., that of prediction. However, it should be clear that the answers to this question would greatly aid future attempts at prediction.

5. It is impossible to say what effect(s) sample attenuation has had. It seems reasonable to assume that one effect will be for our data to be conservative. That is, we will probably underestimate the negative changes that have taken place. Obviously the marriages that ended in divorce are not included. But, less extreme than this, it also seems reasonable to expect that spouses who are very unhappy (but not divorced) would be less likely to continue to respond.

6. Burgess and Wallin, op. cit.

7. Respondents were asked their education only in the engagement schedule. It is virtually certain that more husbands and wives reached this level by the early years.

8. We shall explore the occupational mobility patterns of these couples in detail below. See Chapter Three.

9. Burgess and Wallin, op. cit., Chapter 18; also see Ernest W. Burgess, Harvey J. Locke, and Mary Margaret Thomas, The Family (New York: American Book Company, 1963, third edition), Chapter 15.

10. Burgess and Wallin, op. cit., pp. 592-93.

11. The attached appendix contains a complete inventory of all items involved in this and the other measures used here.

12. The responses taken as traditional for these five items are as follows: 1) yes; 2) no; 3) yes; 4) no; 5) yes.

13. Lee Rainwater, Family Design (Chicago: Aldine Press, 1964), pp. 28-40; also see Elizabeth Bott, "Conjugal Roles and Social Networks," in Norman W. Bell and Ezra F. Vogel, (eds.), The Family (Glencoe, Ill.: The Free Press, 1960), pp. 248-57.

14. Rainwater, op. cit., p. 30.

15. This term, of course, comes from Burgess and Locke. See the comments and definition in Burgess, Locke and Thomas, op. cit., pp. 265-67.

16. Rainwater, op. cit., p. 32.

17. Burgess, Locke and Thomas, op. cit., p. 4.

18. See the discussion of this in Burgess and Wallin, op. cit., pp. 214-26.

19. Peter C. Pineo, "Disenchantment in the Later Years of Marriage," Marriage and Family Living (1961), 23:3-11. This article is taken from a dissertation by the same author. See his Dyadic and Change Analysis in a Study of Marriage and Divorce, unpublished Ph.D. dissertation, University of Chicago, Department of Sociology (1960).

20. Ibid., p. 7.

21. Ibid., p. 8.

II
PATTERNS OF CHANGE: GROWING APART

It is not surprising that, early in marriage, the typical husband-wife relationship in our sample of couples was egalitarian, both in terms of the ideals expressed by husband and wife and in terms of the actual role relationships they had elaborated. Husbands no doubt helped around the house; wives, as we shall see later, helped augment their husbands' income and, in general, the differentiation between husband and wife was rather low. The primary basis for this equality, aside from the fact that husband and wife desired it, was undoubtedly the fact that both husband and wife, in substantial measure, saw "eye to eye." With no serious disagreements to resolve, there was little need for one or the other spouse to assume a commandeering position over the other--and few assumed such a role. Intimately connected with this egalitarian relationship, probably in part a basis for it and certainly a resultant of it, is the general warmth of the husband-wife relationship: husbands and wives, for the most part, were happy, thought well of one another and expressed love for one another, and had given no thought whatever to either divorce or separation. The predominant type of husband-wife relationship very closely approximates what Burgess has called the "companionate family"--a consensual, egalitarian and affectionate husband-wife relationship.[1] But, like all social relationships, this changes. In this chapter, we shall examine the changes that took place in these 400 marriages.

By the middle years of marriage (fifteen years after the early years), quite startling changes had taken place. Before examining some of the specific dimensions of these changes, let us look first at the general indicator, the marital adjustment score. Where once the vast majority of husbands and wives reported high levels of adjustment, by the middle years of marriage, appreciable numbers of husbands and wives indicated that their adjustment to one another had worsened.[2] To be more precise, over two-thirds of the spouses scored lower on the MAS in the middle years than they had in the early years of marriage (see Table 2-1).

Table 2-1.--INITIAL LEVEL OF AND SUBSEQUENT CHANGE IN MARITAL ADJUSTMENT: HUSBANDS AND WIVES

Initial level of adjustment	Change in adjustment			Total	Number of cases
	Increase	No change	Decrease		
Husbands					
High............	21.6	1.0	77.3	100.0	194
Moderate.........	38.1	3.2	58.8	100.0	160
Low.............	44.2	2.3	53.5	100.0	43
Number of cases..	122	8	267		397
Wives					
High............	24.4	1.8	73.8	100.0	221
Moderate.........	33.8	1.4	64.8	100.0	145
Low.............	44.1	...	55.9	100.0	34
Number of cases..	118	6	276		400

Pineo's earlier analysis of change in these couples revealed that loss of adjustment was the most predominant change.[3] Terming this declining adjustment "disenchantment," he suggested that what was involved was, essentially, a "regression effect" in which the extremes of adjustment were leveled out, meeting at some theoretical mean point. This, for Pineo, was the result of mate selection which, in our society, results in a maximization of "fit" between husband and wife at the time of marriage. As a result of this maximization, decline is the only possible direction change can take. Presumably, where the "fit," for whatever reasons, is not maximized--i.e., poor marital adjustment--change will be in the direction of improvement (or the marriage will be broken). Table 2-1 shows clearly that the higher the level of initial adjustment, the greater the likelihood of subsequent decline.[4] On the face of it, this confirms Pineo's line of reasoning. However, what Pineo neglects is that regardless of initial level of adjustment, the majority of husbands and wives suffered decline in level of adjustment. Clearly, this is not simply a change built into the mate selection process; nor does it seem that husbands and wives are simply regressing to a theoretical mean level of adjustment. For this to be the case, most of the spouses with initially low levels of adjustment would have had to increase in order to meet those well adjusted husbands and wives who are losing ground. We shall have to examine the substantive meaning of the adjustment of husband to wife (and vice versa) for an explanation of this change.

As we noted in Chapter One, the marital adjustment index basically involves a series of questions designed to measure the extent to which husbands and wives are able to get along comfortably with one another--the more sharing, the greater the expressed happiness, the less quarreling, and so forth, the higher one scores on the index. All of these factors involve a more or less complete submission of individual will to the needs of the couple: a togetherness. This, of course, is what marriage is supposed to be in our society. The honeymoon is a dramatic symbolization of this: the newlyweds retreat into seclusion and, for a short time, society relinquishes its claims on the husband and wife as individuals[5]; and it is during this time that the newlyweds are expected to begin to build a firm sense of unity into their relationship. The isolation of the honeymoon obviously does not last very long but, as we have seen, the companionate style of relationship persists at least through the first few years of marriage. Having established a joint role relationship, husband and wife act as a unit--they work together and play together and little separates them.

With time, however, new demands are made of the husband and wife such that more distinct husband and wife spheres of activity may come into being. One very natural demand of this sort results from the birth of children. Other studies have indicated that children tend to reduce husband-wife adjustment.[6] In our sample we find a slight tendency for children to be disruptive of adjustment (see Table 2-2).

Table 2-2.--NUMBER OF CHILDREN AND PERCENT OF HUSBANDS AND WIVES DECREASING IN MARITAL ADJUSTMENT

Number of children		Percent decrease in marital adjustment		Total
Initially	Added	Husbands	Wives	
0	2 or fewer	63.8	66.6	105
0	3 or more	76.6	70.2	47
1	1 or fewer	66.7	69.5	99
1	2 or more	66.3	75.4	110
2-3	1 or fewer	79.0	57.9	19
2-3	2 or more	64.7	70.6	17

However, this is most clearly the case for wives. For the wife, regardless of the number of children present at the time of the early years interview, the greater the number of children born subsequent to that first interview, the greater the likelihood that the wife will decrease in adjustment.[7] With husbands, this is true only in those cases where there were either no children present at the time of the first interview or where there already were several; adding more children is less disruptive for the husbands than is the addition of few children.

The fact that large increments in the number of children are more disruptive for the wife than for the husband suggests to us that children set the stage for a shift in the balance that husband and wife initially develop in their relationship. Typically, wives withdraw from the labor force. Concomitant with this, the wife begins to assume tasks that the husband can (or will) share only sporadically. The shift from wife to wife-mother also means an alteration in the objects of her attention with her focus increasingly directed to the home and home related activities. While the wife makes these adjustments, the husband is expected to carry on much as before. He is usually excused from work for a day or two after the birth of a child but is required to resume his responsibilities as breadwinner very quickly. In other words, the high degree of similarity in husband-wife activities is placed under a strain--if not made impossible--as the family grows in size and, as we shall try to demonstrate, husband and wife tend to grow apart.

This is not to place the burden of decreasing marital adjustment on children. The relationship between size of family and adjustment, judging from others' work, is neither simple nor direct, rather, it is contingent upon a number of additional factors, e.g., husband-wife desires for children, which we need not explore here since our major interest lies elsewhere.[8] And on the basis of our own data, as presented in Table 2-2, it is clear that the differences resulting from small and large additions to the family are quite small, far too small to suggest that children, no matter how many, are a major source of the attenuation of adjustment reported by husbands and wives. But we are not especially interested in causes at this point. What is suggested is that declining adjustment represents a change in the relationship between husband and wife, a change that involves movement from a joint role relationship to a more segregated role relationship.[9] Having made this assertion, let us now examine in detail the changes that took place in the role relationships between husband and wife and the relationship between these changes and the changes we have observed in marital adjustment.

Changes in Roles: From Joint to Segregated Organization

Essential to the maintenance of any reciprocal relationship, regardless of the particular allocation of roles, is the continued existence of agreement as to what each participant should do--the roles to be played and the values to be maximized. Without this basic agreement, the likelihood that serious conflict will occur increases, as does the likelihood of disruption of communication between spouses. In the early years, as we have noted several times, our couples enjoyed substantial consensus on the running of the household. By the middle years, however, marked decline in husband-wife agreement was reported by both spouses. Specifically, 58 percent of the husbands and 58 percent of the wives indicated that agreement on such vital matters as the handling of finances, rearing of children and relationships with in-laws had declined since early marriage (see Table 2-3). While the maintenance of consensus is crucial to any sustained interaction of persons, it is clear that the companionate--or jointly organized--marital relationship is especially dependent upon husband-wife agreement on how the family should be run. Given the heavy emphasis on commonality and shared responsibility extant in such relationships, the failure to sustain consensus can only indicate that husband and wife, for one reason or another, come to face a divergence of interest and opinion. That this divergence poses a real threat to the couple's ability to smoothly and pleasurably share family activities and responsibilities hardly needs stating. The pronounced relationship between declining consensus and declining adjustment, shown in Table 2-3, makes this amply clear.

Table 2-3.--CHANGES IN CONSENSUS AND MARITAL ADJUSTMENT FOR HUSBANDS AND WIVES

Change in consensus	Change in marital adjustment		Total	Number of cases
	Increase	Decrease		
Husband				
Increase...	55.9	44.1	100.0	143
Stable.....	25.0	75.0	100.0	20
Decrease...	16.5	83.5	100.0	224
Total number of cases....	122	265		387
Wife				
Increase...	50.7	49.3	100.0	147
Stable.....	30.0	70.0	100.0	20
Decrease...	16.7	83.3	100.0	228
Total number of cases....	118	267		394

The decline in husband-wife consensus and the relationship this decline has to the general loss of adjustment of husband and wife begins to provide us with some insight into the changes in the husband-wife relationship. First of all, stated baldly, the relationship tends to become more conflictful. For whatever reasons, husbands and wives, over time, tend to increasingly differ over the ways each feels the other should carry out key familial duties. Under these circumstances, it seems reasonable to expect that husband and wife would begin to alter the allocation of roles so as to minimize the amount of open conflict. To take a hypothetical though not improbable example, if husband and wife begin to disagree over the handling of children, they may decide, formally or otherwise, to leave that job to only the wife. In one study of child rearing, for example, it was noted that, with each successive birth, the husband participates less and less in the training of the child.[10] Unfortunately, no attempt was made to see to what extent the withdrawal of the husband from this activity was due to disagreements with the wife on how the training of children should be handled. In any event, this does not appear too unlikely a reason for a husband's withdrawal.

Another important possibility to consider, and one for which we have data, is that under conditions of declining consensus the authority relations of husband and wife change. Knowing the distribution of authority, like knowing the degree of consensus, is basic to an understanding of the role relationships between spouses. If this role relationship is to be a jointly organized one, then authority has to be more or less equally distributed--and decisions must be shared--and neither spouse should aspire to dominance. Let us examine the changes that took place in the reports of husband and wife regarding dominance in their relationship.

In the early years of marriage, we saw that spouses tended to shy away from being dominant, few reporting any great desire to take command. The changes that took place are in marked contrast to this initial reluctance to being dominant--husbands and wives, and especially the husbands, tend to report an increased desire to "wear the pants" (see Table 2-4).[11] While it is not particularly surprising

Table 2-4.--CHANGES IN HUSBAND'S DOMINANCE-SUBMISSION SCORE BY CHANGE IN WIFE'S SCORE

Husband	Wife			Total	Number of cases
	Increase	Stable	Decrease		
Total............	49.1	4.5	46.3	100.0	
Number of cases..	196	18	185		399
Increase...........	26.3	2.5	22.0	50.9	203
Stable.............	2.0	0.2	2.8	5.0	20
Decrease...........	20.8	1.8	21.6	44.1	176

to find that the majority of husbands come to desire a larger share in decision-making (for this still is a relatively widespread and accepted masculine prerogative[12]), it is indeed surprising to discover that almost as many wives as husbands increase in dominance. Clearly, in the middle years of marriage husbands and wives no longer individually reject dominance. And, as the data in Table 2-4 indicate, by the middle years of marriage, many couples had moved away from the more or less even distribution of authority that had characterized their marital relationship in the early years.

Looking at this more closely, four types of rearrangements in husband-wife dominance have occurred. In two of these four, husband-wife changes reflect a clear movement away from whatever equality husband and wife enjoyed in the early years: in 24 percent of the couples, movement is toward patriarchy (husband increase and wife decrease); in 23 percent, movement is toward matriarchy (wife increase and husband decrease).[13] In both cases, the joint relationship of the early years is declining. In a purely formal sense, the two remaining types of rearrangement are equalitarian--i.e., both husband and wife change in the same direction. On the one hand, we find 26 percent of the couples have both spouses increasing in dominance and, on the other, 22 percent in which both decrease in dominance. However, the similarity stops at the formal level. In substantive terms, it seems apparent that quite different authority relations are involved in each. Adopting, for the moment, a military metaphor may help us distinguish between the two situations. In the case where both husband and wife increase in dominance, it seems appropriate to see this type of formal equality as a "balance of terror" as opposed to the equality inhering in the situation where both decrease in dominance, akin to "reciprocal disarmament." While these terms no doubt greatly overstate the conditions of husband-wife authority in each of the two instances, it does seem clear that quite different relationships are to be expected in each.

Our interest in movement to or from equality results from a more general interest in the overall role relationship between husband and wife, and the changes in this overall relationship. We started with the general observation that husbands and wives began their marriages with a joint or companionate role relationship. Authority is obviously a central focus in this style of relationship and the authority relationships were not only equalitarian but, of equal importance, were also such that the general level of dominance was low. As the general level of dominance increases, even if equally between husband and wife, it would seem reasonable to expect that basis for joint decision-making and companionship is thereby altered. In other words, we are suggesting that in only those cases where both the husband and wife decreased in dominance can we meaningfully speak of continued or strengthened companionship and joint role organization: all other patterns of change involve movement away from this type of relationship. This can be demonstrated by examining the relationship between changes in dominance and changes in marital adjustment and changes in consensus.

As Table 2-5 demonstrates, changes in dominance contribute to

Table 2-5.--CHANGES IN DOMINANCE AND CHANGES IN ADJUSTMENT FOR HUSBAND'S AND WIVES

Change in dominance	Change in adjustment		Total	Number of cases
	Increase	Decrease		
Husband				
Increase......	26.2	73.8	100.0	195
Decrease......	40.3	59.7	100.0	176
Number of cases.	112	249		371
Wife				
Increase......	22.7	77.3	100.0	194
Decrease......	35.7	64.3	100.0	182
Number of cases.	109	267		376

changes in adjustment and, as expected, the relationship is an inverse one--declines in adjustment are more likely if dominance has increased than if dominance has decreased. While the relationship is not as strong as we would desire, it does indicate that changes in dominance are reflected in more general aspects of the husband-wife relationship and that in those instances where the distribution of authority shifts, companionship between husband and wife suffers.

Of even more importance for assessing the specific nature of the changes in the husband-wife relationship is the interconnection between changes in consensus and changes in dominance, for it is in this that we can most clearly see how husband-wife roles have become reallocated. The general shape of the connection between dominance and consensus is, on the basis of our previous observations, predictable: in those cases where the individual reports increasing consensus, the likelihood of decreasing dominance is greatest. But of more interest to us here than the relationship between changes at the individual level is the effect of changes in husband-wife patterns of dominance and their relationship to husband's and wife's reports of change in consensus.

In those couples in which both husband and wife increase in dominance (the "balance of terror" situation) we find that the likelihood that husband and wife will decline in their estimation of consensus with one another is highest (see Table 2-6). By contrast, consensus

Table 2-6. --PATTERNS OF CHANGE IN DOMINANCE AND CHANGE IN HUSBAND'S AND WIFE'S CONSENSUS

Patterns of changing dominance	Percent decreasing in consensus		Total
	Husband	Wife	
Both increase....	67.6	67.6	105
Husband increase, wife decrease...	51.4	65.2	109
Wife increase, husband decrease	65.3	61.2	98
Both decrease....	50.6	42.4	85

decreases least for those spouses who have, together, declined in dominance. This finding gives clear support to our line of reasoning--only in those cases where both husband and wife decline in dominance does one find joint role organization and companionship enhanced (or at least sustained). But looking only at the two polar types of change in dominance obscures another very important aspect of the relationship between change in dominance and change in consensus. In the cases where husband-wife change in dominance is complementary, where either patriarchy or matriarchy begins to emerge, husband's and wife's consensus are differently affected. For the husband, movement toward patriarchy tends to reduce the likelihood of the husband declining in consensus while, at the same time, the wife's consensus is not greatly enhanced. The opposite of this situation exists, in far less pronounced a fashion, when the wife assumes dominance; this enhances her perception of agreement but not her husband's. In part, clear hegemony of one spouse (when one increases and the other decreases) carries with it a perception of increased accord for the now powerful spouse, indicating to some extent the subjective basis of the consensus measure. The now dominant spouse is, however, misleading himself for his mate appears to be chafing under the bit. Only in those instances where both spouses decline in dominance does one find declining consensus minimized for both husband and wife; in all other cases one, or both, spouses feel left out and disagree with the state of things.

By this time it is clear that one of the reasons for the overwhelming decline in marital adjustment revolves around the increasing difficulty that husbands and wives appear to be having in working (and playing) together. It seems clear that increasing dominance and the concomitant decreasing consensus represent something that goes deeper than commonplace husband-wife "bickering," even though there are, no doubt, some petty grievances involved. The decline in agreement between spouses and the drift away from equality in decision-making strikes at the very roots of the companionately organized marital relationship. Without a large measure of consensus and without a more or less equal sharing of decisions, companionship has little meaning. But, if companionship is giving way, what is it giving way to?

Unfortunately, we have no data which provide us with a directly observable answer to this question. All that we can say directly is that initial companionship has given way to some other style of relationship between husband and wife. However, given the changes in dominance discussed above, it seems reasonable to infer that what has taken place is simply a growing segregation of husband-wife roles. That is to say, for one reason or another (we shall explore several possible explanations in Chapter Four) the husbands and wives appear to be undergoing a differentiation of roles. Where once husband and wife performed roles more or less interchangeably, they now perform more distinctly separate roles. The most obvious pattern of differentiation is that between home and work, the husband becoming primarily responsible for the latter and the wife for the former. Such a transformation in husband-wife role allocations has been noted by Blood and Wolfe in their study of Detroit marriages and has been placed in broader theoretical perspective by Parsons.[14] However, Blood and Wolfe and Parsons fail to see what, for our couples, seems to be an essential aspect of this transformation: in the process of segregating roles, qualitative changes take place in the marital relationship, changes that make for increasing conflict, conflict that is increasingly serious in the estimation of husband and wife. With increasing specialization, husband and wife apparently find themselves holding divergent expectations regarding the ways family responsibilities should be executed. Husband and wife do not appear to be willing to content themselves with specialties. Although the segregation of roles may be inevitable (we shall argue ultimately that, with marriage at least, this is not necessarily so) and functionally more efficient, it also appears to carry with it certain costs in the form of increased conflict.

One reason for the failure of husbands and wives to accept peaceably this rearrangement and separation of roles, rational though it may be, may lie in the images held by each of what a marriage should "look like." Early marriage, it will be recalled, was typified by husband and wife holding an image of the marital relationship as one in which husband and wife did things together--where no one was dominant and traditional images of marriage and family were devalued. What happened to this image? As these marriages became more traditional--i.e., as roles took on more and more the quality of traditional male-female separation--both husband and wife became less traditional in their views about what marriage should be (see Table 2-7). That is, values and actualities diverged. Not only had the husband-wife relationship changed from what it once was, the change was in a direction opposite to the direction they would have liked to have seen.

Table 2-7. --CHANGES IN TRADITIONALISM: HUSBAND AND WIFE

Change in traditionalism	Husband	Wife
Total......	100.0	100.0
Number of cases.....	386	398
Increase.......	23.8	27.9
Stable.........	14.2	15.1
Decrease.......	61.9	57.0

Thus far, we have concentrated on the changes that took place in the organization of husband-wife roles. Most couples appeared to be moving toward a more segregated role relationship and this movement is related to the more general losses observed in the adjustment of husband and wife. Now, in the face of increasing role specialization, given its relationship to losses in adjustment, what happens to the levels of gratification and commitment of husband and wife? How have they changed and is this change related to the changes in adjustment, consensus and dominance that we have been examining?

Change in Gratification and Commitment

Happiness enjoys a rather unique position in the sociology of marriage in that both the sociologist and the married couples alike agree that it is an important criterion for the "successful marriage."[15] By this criterion, as we noted in Chapter One, most husbands and wives felt their marriages to be successful; perhaps not as successful as could be the case but quite successful enough to sustain commitment to the marriage. By the middle years of marriage, however, a by now familiar change had taken place: 50 percent of the wives and virtually 50 percent of the husbands reported losses in happiness (see Table 2-8).[16] This is truly an unhappy finding in every

Table 2-8.--CHANGES IN HUSBAND'S AND WIFE'S HAPPINESS

Change in husband's happiness	Change in wife's happiness			Total	Number of cases
	Increase	Stable	Decrease		
Total percent	37.9	11.6	50.5	100.0	
Number of cases.......	151	46	201		398
Increase........	21.4	4.0	14.3	39.7	158
Stable..........	4.8	2.8	4.0	11.6	46
Decrease........	11.8	4.8	32.2	48.7	194

sense of the word. However, not only do many husbands and wives report losses in happiness with their marriages, it is also important to note in Table 2-8 that a substantial number of husbands and wives (43.7 percent) do not change in the same direction. That is, in some couples, the husband reports increases in happiness while the wife reports decreases (or vice versa). We shall return to a consideration of this divergence in husband-wife happiness and its meaning in terms of the other changes we have noted above; for the moment, however, it will suffice to simply note that, for both husband and wife, declining happiness is the rule, not the exception.

That the majority of husbands and wives report declining happiness with their marriages indicates that what we have termed growing apart carries with it a decline in the gratification spouses receive from one another--i.e., the quality of the relationship is altered. While quality of relationship is an extremely subjective thing, there are, in our culture, several important dimensions of quality that most people recognize. One such dimension is love. However love is thought of by a given individual, there can be little doubt but that it centers very highly among those qualities that a "good" marriage should have. Noting the changes in the love one spouse feels for the other, then, should provide us with a clearer picture of the extent to which the quality of the marital relationships we are dealing with has changed.

Not surprisingly, husband-wife love for one another tends to decline and, as would be expected, this decline is highly related to declining husband-wife happiness (see Table 2-9). What we suggest is occurring here is a leveling or deadening of the emotional content of the husband-wife relationship. This is not to say that the emotional content of these relationships has become either leveled or deadened; rather, all we are pointing out is that change for most is in this

Table 2-9.--CHANGES IN LOVE AND CHANGES IN HAPPINESS FOR HUSBAND AND WIFE

Change in happiness	Change in love			Total	Number of cases
	Increase	Stable	Decrease		
Husband					
Increase......	46.2	25.3	28.5	100.0	158
Stable........	19.6	39.1	41.3	100.0	46
Decrease......	20.6	13.9	65.5	100.0	194
Number of cases.	122	85	191		398
Wife					
Increase......	33.1	33.1	33.8	100.0	151
Stable........	30.4	37.0	32.6	100.0	46
Decrease......	13.3	14.3	72.1	100.0	203
Number of cases.	91	96	213		400

direction.

Several studies of change in husband-wife relationships, utilizing a much shorter time span than that involved here, have found a tendency for such emotive responses as love to begin to decline shortly after marriage.[17] This phenomenon, sometimes referred to as disillusionment, is typically seen in terms of a realistic reappraisal of one's spouse in light of the new aspects of the spouse revealed by the intimacy of marriage. Surely, though, husband and wife should have discarded ill-conceived illusions long before the time of our middle years interview. Do high levels of love, at the outset of marriage, really set the stage for subsequent "reality shocks" and downward revisions in gratification? No. When we examine the relationship between early years' love and the subsequent changes in happiness, we find no relationship--those who loved their spouses highly in the early years were no more likely than those who loved but moderately to decline in happiness.[18] This, and the fact that changes in love are highly related to changes in happiness, suggests that the changes in both are due less to static aspects of the husband-wife relationship in the early years and are much more the result of the ongoing interaction of husband and wife and the emergent properties of this interaction. This conclusion is buttressed by the fact that changes in love are not related to length of marriage.[19]

Another important aspect of the emotional content of the husband-wife relationship involves the extent to which husband and wife idealize one another. Happy marriages are characterized not only by mutual feelings of warmth and love but also by spouses holding one another in high regard.[20] As with happiness and love, husband and wife both tend to report less idealization for their mates in the middle years than they did in the early years. Specifically, 46 percent of the husbands and 59 percent of the wives declined in the extent to which they idealized their mates. And again we find a close relationship between declining happiness, declining love and declining idealization.[21] In other words, spouses who decrease in happiness also tend to suffer decreasing love and decreasing idealization of their mates.

There can be little doubt, after observing the changes that took place in happiness, love and idealization, that many of the 400 marriages we are examining have become less gratifying for husband and wife. While this is obviously important to an understanding of the general dynamic of the husband-wife relationship, we wish to go one important step further and discover if the decline in personal gratification carries over to changes in the individual's general commitment to his or her marriage. At one level, the question of commitment was answered before we began this analysis in that, in order to remain in the study, husband and wife had to remain married to one another. This is, obviously, prima facie evidence that husband and wife maintained commitment to their marriage. In the absence of such clear cut evidence of a loss of commitment as would be provided by actual divorce or separation, we are forced to rely on husband's and wife's responses to questions asking them about the seriousness with which they have considered taking action on divorce or separation proceedings.

Unlike the patterns of change in happiness, love and idealization, the changes in permanence are not as overwhelmingly negative; neither divorce-minded husbands nor divorce-minded wives (those who report increasingly serious consideration of separation and/or divorce) are in the majority (see Table 2-10). Slightly more than

Table 2-10.--CHANGE IN HAPPINESS AND CHANGE IN PERMANENCE FOR HUSBAND AND WIFE

Change in happiness	Change in permanence			Total	Number of cases
	Increase	Stable	Decrease		
Husband					
Increase......	19.6	55.1	25.3	100.0	158
Stable........	10.9	63.0	26.1	100.0	46
Decrease......	10.8	40.2	49.0	100.0	194
Number of cases.	57	194	147		398
Wife					
Increase......	17.2	56.7	26.5	100.0	151
Stable........	10.9	54.4	34.8	100.0	46
Decrease......	8.9	37.0	54.2	100.0	203
Number of cases.	49	185	166		400

40 percent of the wives and 37 percent of the husbands indicated giving more serious consideration to separation and/or divorce over the course of this study. Of course, even this magnitude of downward movement, while less startling than declines affecting 50 percent and more of the husbands and wives, bespeaks a deterioration in husband-wife relationships of not insignificant proportions. The lower magnitude of decline in permanence also underscores a caveat we have repeatedly entered in discussing the declines in happiness, love and idealization--viz., we are not dealing with absolutes but, instead, movement from one position toward another. That is, we

can only speak of declining happiness, not necessarily of unhappy marriages.

In spite of the lower likelihood of decline in permanence, change in this measure of commitment to marriage is related to the changes we have observed in happiness (see Table 2-10). Although not presented in tabular form, loss of permanence also accompanies declining love and declining idealization. Or, to put it another way, husbands and wives who find themselves, over time, less gratified by their marriage tend to give increasingly serious consideration to ending the marital relationship.

While very few individual husbands and wives, and even fewer couples, experience reductions in all four of the variables we have been dealing with in this section, it does seem reasonable to conclude that, in terms of the emotional quality of the marital relationship and its attractiveness to husband and wife, the general tendency evident in this sample of couples is toward lower levels of emotional response to and gratifications from one's spouse, accompanied by a tendency to give increasingly serious consideration to ending the marriage. With this summary in mind, let us now turn to a consideration of the interaction of changes in measures of husband-wife role structure with the changes in levels of husband-wife gratification and commitment, thereby filling in a general overview of the internal dynamics of the husband-wife relationship.

Role Differentiation, Gratification and Commitment

The preceeding discussion of changes in the relationship between husband and wife has focused on two processes, the movement away from a joint or companionate role organization and declining gratification and commitment, both of which we have seen to be related to the more general tendency for husbands and wives to suffer losses in adjustment. It is now time to ask how these two processes are related to one another. The importance of this question extends beyond the need to round out our empirical description of the changes that took place in the relationships between husbands and wives as they moved from the early to the middle years of marriage. Specifically, an important theoretical issue is involved: to the extent that husbands and wives have actually moved in the direction of an increasing differentiation of their respective roles, there are two quite different hypotheses as to the effects on gratification and commitment. Before examining the empirical relationships involved, let us briefly examine these two hypotheses.

The most theoretically sophisticated treatment of the relationship between role differentiation, gratification and commitment is provided in the work of Parsons and his followers.[22] Following Durkheim, Parsons suggests that there are essentially two modes of integration of social groupings--one based on homogeneity ("mechanical solidarity") and low levels of differentiation and the other based on heterogeneity ("organic solidarity") and consequent high levels of role differentiation. The family, suggests Parsons, tends to be organized along the latter lines owing to the ubiquity of natural lines of differentiation, sex and age, coupled with the normative constraints on husband and wife such that the husband is expected to be the primary breadwinner and the wife is expected to be primarily concerned with organizing the household. The family thus almost necessarily gravitates toward a division of labor based on sex and age differences, taking the resultant interdependencies of family members as the bases upon which integration rests.

On a considerably less deductive basis, Burgess has suggested a quite different situation.[23] Burgess sees an essentially new family form emerging, one that no longer requires a clear division of labor between husband and wife. Rather, the husband-wife bond is coming increasingly to be based upon companionship and homogeneity of activities. Integration (or, for us, gratification and commitment) rests, according to Burgess, on the ability of husband and wife to organize their activities in such a way as to provide for a maximization of common activity and interest--a sharing of decision-making, household tasks and so forth.

In some measure, we have overstated each of these two positions. Parsons admits to the likelihood that complete separation of the husband and wife spheres of activity is inimical to the provision of emotional support in the marriage relationship, which in turn is necessary for its perseverence. Burgess also admits that there are limits to complete uniformity of husband-wife activity and, as a result, some differentiation is necessary for smooth functioning. However, it is clear that Parsons and Burgess emphasize quite different qualities of marital relationship. And, on the basis of the data already presented, it is clear that each position has its empirical justifications. In terms of what actually occurs, with time, in the role relationship of husbands and wives, we have seen that most couples do in fact seem to gravitate to a more differentiated role relationship. But in terms of what husbands and wives want of their marriages, it is also clear that they hold rather firmly to the ideal of companionship, as Burgess suggests they would. More broadly, though, the empirical veracity of each of these two positions rests on the relationship between role differentiation and integration. If Parsons' analysis is correct, we would expect that increasing role differentiation leads to increasing integration--increases in gratification and commitment. If Burgess' analysis is correct, we are led to expect the opposite--increasing differentiation, by reducing companionship, interferes with and militates against the sustaining of close emotional bonds, thereby undermining the integration of husband and wife. Let us examine the data.

The most direct evidence we have on this issue is that involving the relationship between changes in dominance and changes in the spouses' feelings of happiness, love, idealization and permanence. In each instance, the data reveal that movement away from an egalitarian relationship results in disproportionate losses in happiness, love, idealization and permanence. For illustrative purposes, we will focus on two of these four relationships, those involving happiness and permanence since, as noted above, changes in love and idealization virtually duplicate changes in happiness. Table 2-11 presents the data pertinent to these two aspects of marriage, gratification and commitment.

Table 2-11.--CHANGE IN PATTERNS OF DOMINANCE AND CHANGES IN HUSBAND'S AND WIFE'S HAPPINESS AND PERMANENCE

Change in dominance	Happiness		Percent change in opposite direction	Permanence		Number of cases
	Percent decrease			Percent decrease		
	Husband	Wife		Husband	Wife	
Both increase......	61.9	60.0	40.0	47.8	46.7	105
Husband increase, wife decrease.....	47.7	57.8	46.8	45.0	44.0	109
Wife increase, husband decrease..	45.9	38.8	51.0	28.6	34.7	98
Both decrease......	37.6	44.7	36.5	28.2	38.8	85

Looking first at the changes in happiness, two important features bear commenting on. Movement toward egalitarian marriage (both husband and wife decrease in dominance) is generally the least likely to produce declines in happiness, with one exception. In couples where the wife has increased in dominance but the husband has decreased, the wife is the least likely to suffer reductions in happiness. However, her gains are slight over those of the wives in couples where declining dominance is mutual. Beyond this general observation, however, lies an important consideration that allows us to sharpen our formulation considerably. For the husbands especially, role differentiation does seem to be of some help. That is, in the situation where both husband and wife increase in dominance, we cannot speak, legitimately, of increasing role differentiation since both husband and wife appear to be competing for dominance. Only where movement of husband and wife is toward the hegemony of one over the other can we clearly refer to increasing differentiation. Movement toward a more differentiated husband-wife relationship reduces the likelihood of the husband declining in happiness but does not reduce this likelihood to the extent that mutual decline in dominance does. Differentiation, for the husband, is apparently an intermediate type of condition, not the most disruptive and not the least disruptive of happiness. For the wife, one style of differentiation of authority roles is productive of happiness for her--when she moves toward the assumption of control; differentiation in the direction of husband control is quite as disruptive of her happiness as the failure to differentiate. On balance, it seems safe to assert that differentiation of authority roles, relative to movement toward non-competitive equalitarianism--i.e., companionship--is not especially integrative or gratifying to either husband or wife.

The full impact of differentiation in authority becomes even clearer when we consider its effect on the changes in husband-wife happiness. Earlier we noted that a substantial number of husbands and wives tend to change their ratings of happiness in different directions--i.e., if one increases, the other decreases. An examination of Table 2-11 reveals that this tendency for divergence in husband-wife happiness is most marked in those couples that have moved toward increased differentiation and it is least in those marriages in which husband and wife have moved toward companionship. Of what significance is this? What we suggest is simply that movement toward differentiation upsets whatever initial companionship existed, thereby undermining the shared bases of husband-wife happiness. As husband and wife move further apart in terms of the roles they come to play, that which makes one happy (or unhappy) is less likely to make the other happy (or unhappy). Husband and wife, as they undergo movement toward differentiation, come to react to and evaluate the same things differently.

The changes, and their interrelationships, that we have been dealing with thus far coincide with those found by Blood and Wolfe in their study of Detroit families although they did not attempt to uncover the interrelationships we are now examining.[24] Specifically, they noted three trends, proceeding from the honeymoon stage of the family life cycle to the "unlaunched" stage (grown children still at home): 1) the differentiation of husband-wife roles increased, 2) satisfaction with companionship decreased, and 3) satisfaction with love decreased.[25] Their failure to examine the possible interrelationships between these three phenomena is based, we feel, on an implicit assumption: role differentiation is integrative.[26] Their own data cast doubt on the usefulness of this assumption; ours casts even further doubt on the merits of this notion.

Turning now to a consideration of the effect of differentiation on husband's and wife's commitment to marriage, we find results very similar to those just discussed. One major difference stands out:

differentiation leading toward increasing wife dominance appears least likely (no. more likely than when both husband and wife decrease in dominance in terms of husband's permanence) to be disruptive of husband's and wife's permanence (see Table 2-11). While the results are more equivocal in this regard, the major conclusion still seems to lead in the opposite direction.

Before we conclude our remarks on the changes in the husband-wife relationship and turn to a consideration of changes in the external relationships of husband and wife, a brief examination of the relationships between changes in consensus and changes in happiness and permanence is warranted. Consensus, it will be recalled, is a measure of the amount of agreement each spouse perceives with regard to the way decisions should be made and activities carried out. In this sense, the changes in consensus provide us with information on how smoothly the couple is operating and how well each spouse feels roles are being performed. Predictably, decreases in consensus are related to both decreasing happiness and decreasing permanence (see Table 2-12). Since loss of consensus is also related to

Table 2-12.--CHANGE IN CONSENSUS AND CHANGE IN HAPPINESS AND PERMANENCE

Change in consensus	Percent decreasing in happiness	Percent decreasing in permanence	Number of cases
Husband			
Increase.......	40.0	25.3	150
Decrease.......	55.1	44.9	227
Wife			
Increase.......	39.7	32.9	146
Decrease.......	57.7	45.7	234

differentiation (see Table 2-6 above), the relationship between loss of happiness and permanence and declining consensus lends further support to the interpretation we are advancing.

Over time, what seems to be occurring in the majority of the 400 marriages is a movement toward increasingly separate and distinct husband and wife spheres of activity. As a result, husband and wife come to share fewer and fewer tasks and activities. For example, authority tends to become monopolized by one or competed for by both. As spheres overlap less, the bases upon which husband and wife had initially developed a working consensus begin to break down. Criteria for evaluation of role performance and bases of happiness also tend to become distinguished along husband-wife lines. Conflicts and declines in happiness are manifested disproportionately under these circumstances and, ultimately, they find expression in increasingly serious consideration, by both husband and wife, of divorce and/or separation. In other words, husbands and wives seem to be growing apart, their roles becoming distinct and the emotional involvements leveled.

As we suggested in Chapter One, relationships internal to the nuclear family are only one aspect of family life. Each couple exists in and is related in various ways to a broader network of social relationships. There is a public and a private family life and the two interact. We would like now to turn to a consideration of the changes that have taken place in the public--i.e., external--life of our 400 couples. Upon completion of this phase of our analysis, we will then, in Chapter Four, proceed to explore the relationships between the internal and external--private and public--lives of these couples in an attempt to understand more fully the changes we have just examined.

FOOTNOTES

1. Burgess, Locke and Thomas, op. cit., p. 4.

2. We have taken as change the difference between the middle years score and the early years score. The problem of measuring change is by no means resolved. We are fully aware of the likelihood that scores on such indices as we are using are subject to variation in response that may or may not reflect true change. To compensate for this, we could have set an arbitrary interval--e.g., plus or minus five points--around the early years score and treat middle years scores falling in that interval as "no change." This, though, would be fully as arbitrary as our decision to treat all differences as meaningful. Thus, while our figures may well contain some cases of spurious change, we are sure that, given the limitations of the instruments, we have excluded no cases of true change.

3. Pineo, op. cit., pp. 6-7.

4. Obviously, some of this effect could result from the finite limits of the index. For persons scoring at either the top or bottom of the scale, change can only be measured if it occurs in one direction. However, empirically no one received either maximum or minimum scores, leaving the direction of change open in either direction.

5. See Philip E. Slater, "On Social Regression," American Sociological Review (1963), 28:339-64, especially 353-57.

6. Burgess and Wallin, op. cit., p. 717.

7. The major effect of children found by Blood and Wolfe was with the fourth child. See Robert O. Blood and Donald M. Wolfe, Husbands and Wives (Glencoe, Ill.: The Free Press, 1960), pp. 156-57.

8. Burgess and Wallin, loc. cit.

9. We were initially led to examine changes in the role structure by the suggestive work of Parsons and Bales. See Talcott Parsons and Robert F. Bales, Family, Socialization and Interaction Process (Glencoe, Ill.: The Free Press, 1955). We shall deal at some length with their interpretation at several points later in this investigation.

10. Bernard Farber, Family Organization and Interaction (San Francisco: Chandler, 1965), pp. 453-55.

11. As with the consensus measure, we are not presenting changes relative to initial score. All measures we deal with here follow the same pattern as that discussed with the marital adjustment score and there seems to be no need to simply repeat our earlier comments.

12. Blood and Wolfe, op. cit., pp. 44-46.

13. It needs to be emphasized that we are not dealing here with absolutes. We are not interested in whether or not matriarchy, patriarchy or equality are realized. We are only interested in the direction of movement toward or away from any of these conditions.

14. Blood and Wolfe, op. cit., pp. 68-72; Parsons and Bales, op. cit., pp. 23-33.

15. George Levinger, "Marital Cohesiveness and Dissolution: An Integrative Review," Journal of Marriage and Family Living (1965), 27:21.

16. The relationship between change in happiness and change in adjustment is strong. Fifty-three percent of the husbands who increased in happiness decreased in adjustment as compared to 80 percent decreasing in adjustment

among those decreasing in happiness. The figures for wives are 47 percent and 89 percent, respectively.

17. Cf. Charles W. Hobart, "Disillusionment in Marriage and Romanticism," Marriage and Family Living (1958), 20:156-62: also E. E. LeMasters, "Holy Deadlock: A Study of Unsuccessful Marriages," Midwest Sociologist (1959), 21:86-91.

18. However, as with all the other variables, early years level of love is related to changes in love--the higher the initial score, the greater the likelihood of decrease. See footnote 4 above.

19. We arranged the marriages in terms of their length as of the middle years interview. Very few had been married less than 16 years (5 percent) and only two couples had been together more than 20 years. Within this narrow range there were no significant differences in changes in love. In the "youngest" marriages (16 years or less), 54 percent declined in love; in the oldest (20 or more years), the same percentage, 54, declined. This is some indication that, within these limits, length of marriage makes no difference--change is due to factors other than time alone.

20. Levinger, op. cit., p. 21.

21. Of the husbands increasing in idealization, 42 percent decreased in happiness (40 percent decreased in love). Of those decreasing in idealization, 58 percent decreased in happiness (58 percent also decreased in love). For the wife, the respective figures are: 39 percent decrease in happiness (44 percent decrease in love); 58 percent decrease in happiness (60 percent decrease in love).

22. See Parsons and Bales, op. cit., pp. 22-29; also their Chapter Seven.

23. Burgess, Locke and Thomas, op. cit., pp. 265-83. For a comparison of Parsons' and Burgess' positions along the same lines as used here, also see Farber, op. cit., pp. 291-300.

24. Blood and Wolfe attempted to approximate a longitudinal design by ordering their cross-sectional sample into life cycle phases. Thus, the data we are dealing with and their data are not strictly comparable. However, the coincidence is striking nonetheless.

25. Blood and Wolfe, op. cit. For the data on each of these points, see 1) pp. 70-71; 2) p. 156; 3) p. 232.

26. At one point, Blood and Wolfe make this assumption explicit: "Now they (middle aged couples) can express their love through each one's separate contribution to a complementary whole. Marriage can now be symbiotic without having to be synchronous all the time." Ibid., p. 70.

III
HUSBAND AND WIFE IN THE COMMUNITY

Having examined the patterns of change that marked the husband-wife relationship, we will now turn our attention to another facet of the lives of husband and wife. It is obvious that, save for extraordinary circumstances, no couple is immune or oblivious to the demands of the broader social networks within which they work and socialize. It is our intention to examine the ways in which the husbands and wives in our sample altered their involvements in the communities they lived in. Due to limitations of available data, our discussion shall be limited to considerations of, first, the occupational involvements of husband and wife, and second, an examination of their organizational and religious involvements. Ideally, we should also investigate changes in the many possible informal relationships with friends and relatives. However, this information was unfortunately not obtained. Obviously, we are not interested in community participation per se; our primary concern is to discover the relationship(s) between changes in community involvement and changes in the husband-wife relationship. As a result, we will direct attention to those changes in style or degree of community involvement that seem most crucial to the marital relationship.

We have already presented a brief overview of the social backgrounds of the husbands and wives in our sample--essentially middle class backgrounds. By virtue of their social origins, spouses were, in the early years, already substantially involved in their communities. We have noted that the majority of husbands and wives, for example, belonged to at least one organization. Both were typically regular attenders of church and, even at the outset of their careers, husbands were overwhelmingly middle class. It is in this context that we will view change--change that, in most cases, is in the direction of increased involvement in the community. From all appearances, the families we are dealing with have become respectable and, no doubt, respected members in their communities. Central to respected status in the community is, of course, occupation. Let us examine the occupational performance of our couples.

Occupations: Mobility and Success

It is indeed ironic that the same families we have observed growing apart have, in terms of occupational standing, become for the most part very successful. One of the most obvious indications of occupational success is the extent to which sons (the husbands in our sample) and their wives have risen above the occupational levels of their respective fathers. In terms of the broad categories of occupation used in Chapter One, in the early years of marriage, 50 percent of the husbands and wives had gone beyond the occupational status of their fathers.[1] Slightly less than one third of our respondents were at the same occupational level as their fathers' and roughly 13 percent of the husbands started out their careers in occupations ranked below that of their fathers. These figures, in and of themselves, are impressive for they represent, in most cases, the husband's first permanent employment experience. What is more impressive is the fact that when we consider the occupations of the fathers, the majority not lower than the clerical-sales level, we begin to realize that much of the upward mobility we are speaking of is the result of the sons' movement into managerial or professional occupations. Indeed, 83 percent of all sons who were upwardly mobile in early marriage were mobile as the result of their movement into one or the other of these most favored of occupational pursuits. Table 3-1 summarizes these data for the husbands only; the picture for the

Table 3-1.--FATHER'S AND SON'S EARLY MARRIAGE OCCUPATION

Father's occupation	Son's early marriage occupation					Total	Number of cases
	Professional	Managerial	Clerical-sales	Manual	No information		
Professional	76.8	8.7	8.7	4.3	1.4	100.0	69
Managerial	45.7	21.7	21.7	9.8	1.1	100.0	92
Clerical-sales	32.9	22.4	31.8	10.6	2.1	100.0	85
Manual	34.8	19.1	23.6	21.3	1.1	100.0	89
Farm	41.7	12.5	12.5	29.2	4.2	100.0	24
Retired, no information	29.3	39.0	17.1	7.3	7.3	100.0	41
Total number of cases	176	81	84	50	9		400

wives is only slightly altered--a slightly greater proportion of wives were downwardly mobile than husbands. However, even this downward movement involves little crossing of the white collar-blue collar line. Of the 77 wives whose husbands had lower status occupations than the wives' fathers had, 42 (54 percent) had fallen no lower than the clerical-sales level.

But the sons had just begun. While 64 percent of the sons were professionals, managers or proprietors in the early years, the middle years find fully <u>82 percent</u> in these occupations, with only 6 percent remaining in manual occupations. This, regardless of their favorable backgrounds, represents spectacular upward movement in the occupational structure, the more so when one considers the fact that only 36 percent of these sons had fathers in the upper reaches of the occupational world--64 percent of the middle years professionals, managers and proprietors rose above their fathers (see Table 3-2). The picture is no different for the wives: their husbands have provided well for them.

Table 3-2.--FATHER'S AND SON'S MIDDLE YEARS OCCUPATION

Father's occupation	Son's middle years occupation					Total	Number of cases
	Profes-sional	Mana-gerial	Clerical-sales	Manual	No infor-mation		
Professional.......	68.1	23.2	4.3	2.9	1.4	100.0	69
Managerial.........	38.0	45.7	14.1	2.2	...	100.0	92
Clerical-sales.....	34.1	43.5	18.8	3.5	...	100.0	85
Manual.............	34.8	46.1	11.2	6.7	1.1	100.0	89
Farm...............	45.8	29.2	4.2	16.7	4.2	100.0	24
Retired, no information............	26.8	48.8	17.1	4.9	2.4	100.0	41
Number of cases....	164	163	50	19	4		400

However, there are different qualities to be found in mobility of the sort described above. Historically, the significance of occupational mobility has been the result of movement between manual and nonmanual, blue collar and white collar, work. This manual to nonmanual ascent is important because of the changes in attitudes and values usually displayed by those making such shifts.[2] In our sample, however, this type of movement affects only a very small minority of husbands and wives. At the same time, there are other dimensions of mobility that would seem to involve marked changes in attitudes and values of those making the move from one occupation to another. One of these dimensions is clearly type of occupation. Within the white collar segment of the occupational structure, distinctions are emerging between essentially two types of occupations--entrepreneurial and bureaucratic. Several authors have noted that roles in each of these types of occupations are different and each type seems to require substantially different sets of values and attitudes.[3]

Since this distinction is by now a relatively common one, there seems to be no need to go into an elaborate discussion of all the differences between these two types of occupations. For our purposes, it is sufficient to contrast the different meanings attached to mobility in each type of occupational endeavor. With the entrepreneur, mobility involves risks, sometimes great risks. Fortunes are constantly in jeopardy; one week's (or month's or year's) good luck can be transformed into failure as sales fluctuate, prices rise (or fall), and the general state of the economy changes. This is manifested in the rather erratic career lines of those engaged in entrepreneurial occupations--in and out of businesses, changes in sales positions and so forth. All of this connotes something of the unpredictable. In contrast, the bureaucrat can be allowed relatively certain mobility expectations.[4] Much of the risk is taken out of mobility in the bureaucratic occupation. Criteria for advancement are formalized into steps, and, short of the total collapse of the organization, the future is relatively secure. "Good" and "bad" weeks have no impact (or relatively little impact) on remuneration. In short, the husband's ability to plan ahead is greatly enhanced if he chooses a bureaucratic career as opposed to an entrepreneurial career. Movement from one type of occupation to another, then, should carry with it alterations in perspective and style of life.[5] To what extent do we find movement between risk and nonrisk types of occupations?

To answer this question, we attempted to classify the occupations of the husband at the early and middle years and both the husband's and wife's father's occupations. This classification was carried out on a judgmental basis. Each respondent was asked to list his (her) father's occupation and his own present occupation. No detail was requested and little was offered and, as a result, there are many ambiguous cases. The resultant classification can be considered as only a very rough approximation of these two types of occupations but the central idea involved in this classification seems important enough to warrant even so rough an approximation. A complete listing of the occupations of father and son, and their classification into risk and nonrisk types would be too lengthy to present here. However, to give the reader a clearer idea of the empirical content of these two types, the most typical occupations and their classification into types follows:

RISK	NONRISK
salesman	teacher (all levels)
owner of business	minister
lawyer (unless specified as attached to government or corporation)	all blue collar
	doctor
	engineer
accountant (independent)	civil servant
farmer	manager or executive

Even when we consider types of occupations, we find a good deal of movement across generations. Most fathers were to be found in risk occupations but sons tended to gravitate to nonrisk type occupations at the beginning of their participation in the labor force (see Table 3-3). Very crudely, it would seem that this movement reflects the broader changes in the country's occupational structure, changes

Table 3-3.--HUSBAND'S TYPE OF OCCUPATION, EARLY AND MIDDLE YEARS, AND FATHER'S TYPE OF OCCUPATION

Husband's type of occupation, early-middle	Father's type of occupation		Number of cases
	Nonrisk	Risk	
Total.............	100.0	100.0	
Nonrisk-nonrisk.......	45.2	27.5	121
Nonrisk-risk.........	21.5	24.8	83
Risk-nonrisk.........	4.4	4.1	15
Risk-risk............	28.9	43.6	134
Number of cases.......	135	218	353

involving the growth of bureaucratic organizations and the movement away from small, individually owned businesses. For young men entering the labor market in the early 1940's (either before the war or immediately after the war), even for those interested in a business career, the nonrisk occupations were no doubt plentiful. In the early years, approximately 45 percent of the husbands had an occupation different in type from that of their fathers', mostly accounted for by the movement from risk to nonrisk occupations. However, by the middle years many husbands had changed again, this time choosing risk types of occupations. As a result, in terms of type of occupation, husbands came to more nearly resemble their fathers by the middle years.

The initial thrust toward nonrisk occupations and then the reversal indicates several things. First of all, it may well be the case that the husbands just beginning marriage are less likely to take on additional commitments where rewards are uncertain. Further, many, while desiring some kind of self-employment, may simply lack sufficient resources to begin both a household and a business. As a result, at the outset of the career, a safe, regularly paying job may look more attractive. As time goes on, however, capital is accumulated, contacts are made and the husband feels more at ease taking chances. And virtually one quarter of the husbands did just this--they moved from nonrisk to risk types of occupations.

There is, it should be noted, an important characteristic of nonrisk occupations that makes movement out of them easier than movement into them--*viz.*, training. For example, teachers can move into selling quite readily but salesmen cannot, normally, move easily into teaching; not, that is, without additional training. Even in our highly educated sample, husbands in risk occupations are less likely than husbands in nonrisk occupations to have completed at least four years of college. In other words, one of the reasons for a greater percentage of husbands going from nonrisk to risk occupations, compared to those going in the opposite direction, is simply the relatively formal ease of entry into risk types of occupations.

We began the discussion of risk versus nonrisk occupational types on the basis of a distinction between the two along the dimension of predictability of rewards. To round out our discussion of occupational mobility, let us now turn our attention explicitly to the matter of rewards. To say, as we have, that rewards are less certain in risk occupations is not to say that rewards are necessarily lower. While on the average, many of the occupations we have classified as "risk" have lower median incomes than those classified as "nonrisk" (for example, salesmen, in 1960 had a lower median income than teachers), husbands in our sample do not follow this pattern. At the middle years period, husbands in risk occupations made more money than those in nonrisk occupations. They took a chance and made good.

Evidence of the extent to which husbands made good is clearly revealed when we examine the changes in income from early to middle years of marriage. By dividing the middle years income by the early years income, we arrived at a measure of increase--the larger the quotient, the greater the increase. Over 40 percent of all husbands experienced at least a quadrupling of income in the course of this study. Not quite 10 percent increased their income by a factor of eight. During the time span of this study (roughly from 1942-46 to 1955-59), an individual had to nearly double his income in order to keep pace with the changing value of the dollar and the general alterations in wages and prices.[6] Only 7 percent of the husbands failed at least to hold their own in terms of relative purchasing power.

When changes in income are examined in terms of intragenerational changes in type of occupation, it becomes apparent that risk occupations are not, for these men at any rate, unrewarding. The least rewarding in financial terms is the nonrisk career; only slightly more than one quarter of the husbands who began and continued in nonrisk occupations quadrupled their incomes (see Table 3-4). By

Table 3-4.--CHANGE IN HUSBAND'S TYPE OF OCCUPATION AND CHANGE IN HUSBAND'S INCOME

Change in husband's type of occupation early-middle	Change in Husband's Income*				Total	Number of cases
	Decrease	Stable	Moderate increase	High increase		
Nonrisk-nonrisk.......	7.6	64.9	19.8	7.6	100.0	131
Nonrisk-risk..........	5.4	37.6	29.0	28.0	100.0	93
Risk-nonrisk..........	11.1	38.9	33.3	16.7	100.0	18
Risk-risk.............	5.7	43.6	30.0	20.7	100.0	140
Number of cases.......	25	188	101	68		382

* The categories used here represent the following income changes:

Decrease: income less than doubled
Stable: income rose by factor between 2.0 and 3.9
Moderate increase: income rose by factor between 4.0 and 5.9
High increase: income rose by factor of 6.0 or more

contrast, 50 percent of the husbands who began and stayed in risk occupations quadrupled their incomes. And, as we had anticipated, those husbands who moved from nonrisk to risk occupations were the most favored of all--nearly 60 percent of them quadrupled and almost 30 percent at least sextupled their yearly earnings. In spite of these quite marked differences, however, it is clear that the husbands in our sample have done quite well for themselves and their families.

It is clear, that, simply discussing mobility in terms of changes, inter- and intragenerational, in occupation obscures the fact that occupational success, in terms of financial rewards, has been secured by many of the husbands. As a matter of fact, changes in income are not as highly related to the more standard measures of occupational mobility as one would expect. Of those who suffered relative declines in income, 48 percent were upwardly mobile occupationally--i.e., had middle years occupations ranked higher than their early years occupation. Compared to this, 57 percent of those whose incomes increased at least sixfold were upwardly mobile occupationally. Clearly, in whatever terms success is measured, these husbands have secured it: their initial occupations are, generally, above those of their fathers; subsequent changes in the occupational level of the husbands further accentuate this movement beyond their fathers; in terms of income, perhaps the keenest index of success, over 40 percent of the husbands have managed to at least quadruple their incomes.

In our discussion of the couples' relationships to the occupational structure, we have thus far treated the wife as though she were a passive agent. As the following figures indicate, her role has hardly been a passive one: only 14 percent of the wives in our sample have never worked since their marriage; 57 percent have worked at some time during the course of their marriage (typically within the first few years) but were not working at the time of the middle years interview; 28 percent of the wives were working at the time of the middle years interview.[7] Of those wives who had never worked, nearly all gave as their reason for not working the assertion that the "wife's place is in the home." By contrast, only 4 percent of the wives who were working at the time of the middle years interview felt that the wife's place was in the home; the reason given by these wives was, typically, feminist in nature--the response "the wife should have a career since she makes a better companion" was the most common response of the wives then employed. For those who worked at one time but had stopped before the middle years, the most common response, subscribed to by 40 percent of these women, is not surprisingly one of stressing the instrumental value of work--"we needed the money."[8] In other words, at one time or another, most of the wives left their homes and actively assisted their husbands in securing an income for the couple's needs.

Although the vast majority of wives had worked at one time or another since their marriage, husbands were not always pleased with their wives' working. In the early marriage, as a matter of fact, well over half of the husbands indicated objections to their wives' employment but, by the middle years, some husbands had mellowed and the tables were turned--the majority of husbands in the middle years approved of the wife's working. The shift in husbands' attitudes toward wife working is unrelated to the wife's actual working and, interestingly enough, the change is unrelated to husband's mobility. However, the wife is not immune to the pressures of their husband's occupational success. There is a direct relationship between the wife's middle years employment and the changes in her husband's income. While 50 percent of the wives whose husband's income decreased were working in the middle years, only 12 percent of the wives whose husbands' incomes had greatly increased (quadrupled) were working. Thus, it seems that the wife's decision to work depends less on what the husband says and considerably more on what he actually does. In sum, whether or not the husbands know it or like it, it seems clear that their wives have had some direct hand in securing the status of the couples, either by providing an additional thrust as the husband was getting started right after marriage or by continuing a more or less active involvement in the task of adding to the family's income.

We have spent a good deal of time discussing the objective features of the husband's and wife's relationship to the occupational structure of the community in which they live. We have seen that risks were taken by many and, for the most part, were capitalized on by most; we have seen much success and little failure, both in terms of movement between occupations and movement within occupations. But we have not yet seen how husbands and wives perceive these successes.

One would expect that, given such startling patterns of upward mobility, husbands and wives would be quite well satisfied with the husband's job--i.e., they would tend to register fewer complaints about the husband's job at the middle years than were indicated at the early years period. Such, ironically, is not the case, at least not to the extent that one would imagine. Forty-two percent of all husbands and wives indicated more grievances with the husband's job as time went on. In the face of such overwhelming occupational success, it is remarkable that so many husbands and wives grew more dissatisfied with the husband's job. Furthermore, upon examination of the relationship between mobility and change in occupational satisfaction, we find a curvilinear pattern (see Table 3-5). Using change in husband's income as a measure of mobility, we find that the greatest mobility does not result in commensurate gains in satisfaction, especially for the husband. As a matter of fact, both husbands and

Table 3-5.--CHANGES IN HUSBAND'S INCOME AND PERCENT OF HUSBANDS AND WIVES INCREASING IN OCCUPATIONAL SATISFACTION

Changes in husband's income	Percent increase in occupational satisfaction		Number of cases
	Husbands	Wives	
Decreased............	58.3	37.5	24
Stable...............	50.5	52.7	182
Moderate increase.....	59.0	58.0	100
High increase........	45.5	44.2	77

wives appear equally unenamored with the husband's job in those cases where he has greatly increased his income. Husbands and wives, however, depart in their evaluations of the husband's job when he has failed to keep pace with the rise in consumer prices--the husband is quite likely to increase in satisfaction, the wife is quite likely to decrease in satisfaction. The disaffection of husbands and wives with the husband's job, except for the one divergence just noted, parallel one another, sharply increasing with high increases in husband's income. It may well be that husbands who have greatly augmented their incomes have had to do so at great expense--non-monetary expense, obviously. Immense demands on time and energy send the balance of psychic costs and monetary rewards into the red. We shall return to this matter, from a somewhat different vantage point in subsequent chapters.

In spite of the fact that satisfaction with the husband's job does not follow the pattern we would have expected, there can be little doubt but that most husbands and wives are clearly better off than their parents and that they recognize this. In early marriage, a little over 50 percent indicated that their current standard of living was above that of their parents. By the middle years, reflecting the continued upgrading of occupation and income, over two-thirds felt that their standard of living exceeded that of their parents. As one would expect, this perception is not simply subjective--the greater the increase in income, the more likely one is to perceive himself better off than his parents. In short, husbands and wives realize that they have been successful in the world of occupational endeavor.

By way of summary, the following four features of the changes in the relationships of husband and wife to the occupational structure are the most striking:

1. Originating from predominantly middle class background, these couples have greatly solidified their middle class status, moving into the most favored of all occupations--the professions.
2. Whatever the changes in occupation, however, many husbands have managed to markedly increase their incomes, recogniz-

ably moving well beyond the life styles of parents.

3. Wives, with very few exceptions, have had a hand in securing the status of the couples although their employment has been intermittent, and sometimes disparaged.
4. In spite of the quite obvious success, significant numbers of husbands and wives declined in feelings of satisfaction with the husband's job.

Having examined the changing patterns of involvement of husband and wife in the occupational structure of the community, let us now turn to a consideration of the changes in the extent to which husband and wife participate in other aspects of the organized community, specifically looking at religious behavior and organizational memberships.

Religion and Organization in the Lives of Husband and Wife

As one would expect of substantial middle class men and women, the husbands and wives in our sample are heavily involved in the affairs and the religious life of the communities in which they live. Couples in which neither spouse is a member of an organization are rare, but rarer still is the couple in which at least one spouse does not attend church, however irregularly (see Table 3-6). As we noted

Table 3-6.--HUSBAND'S AND WIFE'S CHURCH ATTENDANCE

Husband's church attendance	Wife's church attendance				Number of cases
	Did not go		Did go		
	Do not	Do	Do not	Do	
Did not go					
Do not go....	53.7	26.8	2.4	17.1	41
Do go........	1.9	52.8	5.7	39.6	53
Did go					
Do not go....	7.7	26.9	7.7	57.7	26
Do go........	1.2	12.0	3.1	83.8	259
Number of cases.	28	77	14	260	379

earlier, most husbands and wives in early marriage attended church at least occasionally. By the middle years, few husbands and even fewer wives--17 and 11 percent respectively--can not be found attending religious services once in a while. Moreover, if one spouse is in attendance, the likelihood of the other being there too is quite high--71 percent of the husbands and wives attend church with more or less the same frequency. When we get more exacting and separate casual from regular attenders, we find that 57 percent of all couples attended regularly (three or more times per month) in the early years and have continued this pattern into the middle years. What little alteration in frequency of church attendance there is is in the direction of increased attendance; very few husbands and wives have stopped attending since the early years. In other words, in terms of public behavior, the husbands and wives in this sample were and continue to be "religious" people.

Similarly impressive is the number of husbands and wives who have, since early marriage, increased in organizational activity. Approximately 65 percent of all husbands and wives listed more organizations belonged to in the middle years than in the early years. In 50 percent of the couples, both husband and wife increased their range of memberships (see Table 3-7). For most, this increase

Table 3-7.--CHANGES IN HUSBAND'S AND WIFE'S ORGANIZATIONAL ACTIVITY

Husband's organizational activity	Wife's organizational activity			Total	Number of cases
	Increase	Stable	Decrease		
Total..........	65.8	20.9	13.3	100.0	
Number of cases	258	82	52		392
Increase..........	50.3	9.3	7.1	66.8	262
Stable............	10.1	5.8	3.1	18.9	74
Decrease..........	5.6	5.6	3.1	14.3	56

amounts to joining one or two organizations over and above those belonged to in the early years. However, there are a number of instances in which rather large numbers of organizations were joined--18 percent of the husbands and 14 percent of the wives added four or more organizations to their biographies and, in one instance, a husband reported joining 27 organizations in addition to the three he belonged to in the early years. Obviously even the most energetic of persons could not actively participate in this number of organizations and, as a result, a large number of these memberships are no doubt "paper memberships" only. Unfortunately, spouses were asked only to indicate the number of organizations they held memberships in and no information was asked of the actual participation. Consequently, we are unable to sort out active from "paper" memberships. This lack of precision notwithstanding, it is abundantly clear that the community and its religious and organizational networks had, by the middle years, come to figure highly in the lives of husbands and wives.

Relationships to community organizations, sacred and secular, are affected by a number of factors and in order to better assess the participation we have just described, it would be well to consider two important sources of influence on community involvement: geographic and social mobility. Only 56 of the 400 couples (14 percent) had not moved at least once between the early and middle years and over half had moved two or more times since marriage. In spite of their migrations, however, it appears as though spouses have had little trouble becoming involved organizationally in the new communities and neighborhoods. As the number of moves increases, husbands are only slightly less likely to increase in organizational memberships and wives are slightly more likely to increase in this regard (geographic mobility has no effect on church participation).

Given the educational achievements of husbands and wives, coupled with the high occupational status of the husband, it seems reasonable to assume that no matter what community these couples find themselves in, their social skills and status not only make adjustments easy but also make them sought after since they would lend much prestige--if not talent and energy--to any organization. This is made even clearer when we consider the effects of social mobility on organizational participation--with increased success, husbands and wives, and especially the latter, tend to be more community oriented (see Table 3-8). The most successful husbands, however, depart from

Table 3-8.--CHANGE IN HUSBAND'S INCOME AND CHANGE IN HUSBAND'S AND WIFE'S ORGANIZATIONAL ACTIVITY

Change in husband's income	Percent increasing in organizational activity		Number of cases
	Husband	Wife	
Decrease..........	57.7	53.8	26
Stable............	67.0	62.2	185
Moderate increase.	69.9	69.9	103
High increase.....	58.0	68.2	69
Number of cases...	251	246	383

this pattern, with the percentage of husbands who increase in memberships dropping off markedly. It is quite plausible to hold that in the case of the very successful husband, his commitment to occupational and occupation-related activities is of necessity high. This, apparently, cuts into the time and energy he can devote to more diffuse participation in the community (although success, like geographical mobility, is unrelated to church attendance). The wife of the highly successful husband, it would seem, takes over for her husband, for it is only in the stratum of highly successful couples that the wife is more likely than her husband to increase in organizational memberships. We shall return to this phenomenon in the next chapter.

The overwhelming feature of husband-wife relationships to the community is one of social mobility. It is in this context that the other forms of community involvement are to be best understood for without their success in the occupational world, it is doubtful that we would have found the degree of external involvement that we did. At the outset of this chapter, we indicated the irony of decreasing marital happiness and increasing husband-wife conflict in the face of such occupational success. Having now examined both aspects of this ironical situation separately, we are now in a position to begin our analysis of the relationships between success in the external world and the failure to maintain successful--i.e., happy and harmonious--marital relationships. Hopefully, we will be able to turn irony into some meaningful sociological insight.

FOOTNOTES

1. In making comparisons between wife's status and that of her father's, we shall treat wife's status in terms of her husband's. Thus, we are really dealing with the relationships between the husband's level and the levels of his father and father-in-law.

2. The literature on this subject is far too extensive to do justice to it here. See Sorokin's classic study Social and Cultural Mobility (Glencoe, Ill.: The Free Press, 1959), Part Six.

3. See, for example, David Riesman, et al., The Lonely Crowd (New Haven: Yale University Press, 1950), Chaps. 6 and 15; Daniel Miller and Guy Swanson, The Changing American Parent (New York: John Wiley and Sons, 1958), pp. 197-213.

4. This does not mean that bureaucrats are not as competitive (although there is some evidence of this) or as eager for success as entrepreneurs. Rather, it would seem that phenomena like competition and success involve different things depending upon the context. We are also not suggesting the image of the bureaucratic "drone"--they exist but there are also many "adaptive" bureaucrats (see Morris Janowitz, The Professional Soldier (New York: The Free Press of Glencoe, 1962), pp. 165-68; on the greater regularity of bureaucratic careers, also see Harold L. Wilensky, "Work, Careers, and Social Integration," in S.N. Eisenstadt, ed., Comparative Social Problems (New York: The Free Press of Glencoe, 1965), pp. 313-17.

5. Ibid.

6. United States Bureau of the Census, Statistical Abstract of the U.S., 1964, 85th edition (Washington, D.C.: United States Printing Office, 1964), p. 351.

7. The question on wife's working only asked if she was currently working so it is impossible for us to isolate those wives (if any) who were regularly employed throughout marriage.

8. The following table summarizes these statements:

Wife's attitude toward work	Work experience			Number of cases
	Never	Early years	Middle years	
Careerist. . . .	3.5	13.7	49.1	85
Instrumental . .	5.3	31.1	46.4	174
Taditional. . . .	91.2	35.2	4.5	137
Number of cases	57	227	112	396

IV
MOBILITY, OCCUPATIONAL ROLES AND CHANGES IN THE HUSBAND-WIFE RELATIONSHIP

Given only the knowledge of the occupational and educational backgrounds of the couples in our sample, the fact that so many were upwardly mobile should come as no surprise. Indeed, as the middle class generally moved into the affluence of the 1950's, only the most incompetent or unwilling could fail to move in an upward direction--as long as they were white and possessed education. In other words, upward mobility, in some degree at least, was virtually inevitable. In acting out this perhaps more humble version of the American Dream, these couples entrenched themselves in those very occupational strata that are, in our society, least likely to produce disrupted marriages.[1] In this sense, it is surprising that the changes in husband-wife relationships were, generally, of a negative nature. While mobility was largely inevitable, the marital deterioration we have observed does not appear to be inevitable. It is obvious, and this bears repeating, that the couples we are analyzing have not been disrupted; they are still married and, relative to broken marriages, they may even be happily married. But, for many, levels of happiness came to be lower. In this chapter, we shall attempt to discover why these changes in the husband-wife relationship occurred. As we suggested at the outset of this work, we are primarily concerned with the effects of change in the way husbands and wives relate to the external--i. e., community--structures on the changes in the internal, husband-wife, structure. The obvious point of departure for this analysis is to explore the effects of occupational mobility on husband-wife relationships.

The Impact of Occupational Mobility

A considerable body of research, perhaps the largest on any subject in sociology, has revolved around social stratification and the differences in attitudes and behavior associated with various levels in the stratification hierarchy.[2] In terms of husband-wife relationships, the general essence of the research is the finding that the higher one moves in the class and status hierarchy, the better the adjustment and the greater the happiness of husband and wife.[3] Indeed, much recent literature has suggested that those social skills and attitudes associated with getting and holding high status occupations are the same as, or at least productive of, the skills and attitudes required for a happy marriage.[4]

Social mobility obviously involves moving from one level to another in the class hierarchy. As such, mobility has been traditionally viewed as disruptive since it requires the mobile individual to take on new attitudes and learn new behavior appropriate to his new station.[5] More recently, however, it has been found that not all mobility is equally disruptive and, indeed, some types of mobility may actually be quite the opposite. Specifically, several studies have indicated that only downward mobility is disruptive while upward mobility is at least no worse than no movement at all.[6] With regard to marriage, Roth and Peck have reported finding that spouses who were upwardly mobile before marriage tended to have slightly higher adjustment scores (using Burgess' Marital Adjustment Score) than did those who had remained stable and, more significantly, those who were downwardly mobile before marriage had markedly lower adjustment scores than either the stable or upwardly mobile spouses.[7] Changes in status obviously carry with them changes in the relationship to others in the community but, apparently, only those changes which connote failure, bringing the individual into milieux less favorable to the husband-wife relationship, are injurious to marriage.

On this basis, we would expect to find that in our sample downwardly mobile spouses would be the most likely to suffer unfavorable changes in their marital relationships. This expectation, it should be noted, is not a direct replication of the Roth and Peck study for they were not concerned with changes in marital relationship; the only change they focused on was the premarital change in status vis-a-vis the parents of husband and wife. We will be concerned with two changes: 1) changes in marital relationship and 2) changes in status as this unfolded <u>during</u> marriage. Our measure of mobility will be the difference between father's occupation (for both husband and wife) and the son's occupation at the middle years. (We shall also examine the effects of the intragenerational mobility of husbands shortly.) For measuring changes in marital relationship we shall focus on four variables--dominance, consensus, happiness and permanence. These four variables, it will be recalled, proved to be of critical importance in our analysis of the decline in adjustment, a decline attributed to increasing difficulty over the performance of familial roles (increasing dominance and decreasing consensus) and decreasing gratification and commitment (decreasing happiness and permanence).

Table 4-1.--INTERGENERATIONAL MOBILITY AND CHANGES IN INDICES OF HUSBAND-WIFE RELATIONSHIP

Intergenerational mobility	Dominance Percent of couples, both H and W increase	Consensus Percent decreasing		Happiness Percent decreasing		Permanence Percent decreasing		Number of cases
		Husband	Wife	Husband	Wife	Husband	Wife	
Husband								
Up..........	26.8	59.7	62.1	44.7	49.5	35.9	37.9	206
Stable......	22.3	58.0	56.3	49.1	50.9	39.3	45.2	112
Down........	31.7	53.7	53.7	53.7	51.2	39.0	56.1	41
Wife								
Up..........	25.8	53.8	61.3	47.7	50.8	37.2	40.2	199
Stable......	28.3	63.7	59.3	48.7	54.0	36.3	41.6	113
Down........	30.4	60.9	58.7	52.2	48.9	42.6	46.8	47

Table 4-1 presents the relevant data for assessing the effects of intergenerational mobility of both husband and wife on the four indices of the husband-wife relationship. In all cases, in this and subsequent tables (unless otherwise stated), the percentages should be viewed in terms of negative change--i.e., the larger the percentage, the greater the proportion suffering setbacks in their marital relationship. The results are anything but uniform across the four variables and the differences involved are small. In only one case are the differences at all large: wives of downwardly mobile husbands are much more likely to report increasingly serious consideration of separation and/or divorce. In spite of the small differences, however, it is suggestive to note that, generally, upward mobility produces proportionately fewer husbands and wives who change for the worse than does downward mobility. Aside from this regular but small difference, there is no basis for concluding that intergenerational mobility has any great impact on changes in the husband-wife relationship.

This does not, of course, deny the validity of the findings of Roth and Peck. It may well be that mobility prior to any given point in time (the time of marriage for example) affects the husband-wife relationship at that point in time. Our data simply indicate that when occupational mobility and the marital relationship are viewed developmentally, they bear little relationship to one another. Of course, we are, like Roth and Peck, speaking here of intergenerational mobility--the movement of sons and daughters vis-a-vis their parents. It seems reasonable to assume that large differences between, say, son's and son's father's occupational status are only important for a brief time; as the upward or downward movement becomes more remote in time, as the difference is adjusted to, this difference in status means less for son's (or daughter's) behavior. As a result, for our purposes, husband's early marriage occupation may be a better basis for comparison. While intergenerational mobility seems, for our couples, to be of little importance, intragenerational mobility, because it is more proximate, may be of some help in understanding changes in the husband-wife relationship.

Table 4-2.--HUSBAND'S OCCUPATIONAL MOBILITY, EARLY TO MIDDLE YEARS, AND CHANGES IN INDICES OF HUSBAND-WIFE RELATIONSHIP

Husband's occupational mobility	Dominance Percent of couples, both H and W increase	Consensus Percent decreasing		Happiness Percent decreasing		Permanence Percent decreasing		Number of cases
		Husband	Wife	Husband	Wife	Husband	Wife	
Up	14.5	60.0	63.6	55.4	59.1	37.2	38.2	110
Stable	28.6	59.8	58.5	45.1	48.7	38.0	42.0	226
Down	39.1	54.7	57.8	50.0	47.8	40.6	45.3	64

When the husband's career is examined for upward or downward mobility, we find contradictory relationships between mobility and change in marital relationships (see Table 4-2). First of all, with respect to indices of role conflict, we see that upward mobility is far less likely than either stability or downward mobility to produce a situation where both husband and wife vie for dominance. Although not shown in Table 4-2, what occurs in the couples in which the husband is upwardly mobile is not a mutual decline in dominance (21 percent of the upwardly mobile couples had both husband and wife decreasing in dominance while 17 percent of the downwardly mobile couples were so characterized) but, rather, a very high likelihood of husband being ascendant and wife "giving in." Upwardly mobile couples avoid the most disruptive situation but do not, thereby, move toward equality in authority. This is reflected in the changes in husband's and wife's alterations in consensus. While the differences are small, upwardly mobile couples are the most likely to be couples in which husbands and wives decrease in consensus. In other words, upward mobility, which, in this sample, means movement into professional and managerial occupations, is the least likely to lead to open power struggles between husband and wife, but it is the most likely to lead to a situation in which husband and wife segragate their roles; as a result, upward mobility does not seem to facilitate improved husband-wife agreement over the performance of family roles. Upward mobility is, in short, not an unmixed blessing.

Further evidence of the mixed effect of mobility can be seen in the relationship between mobility and the indices of husband-wife gratification. While upward mobility of the husband leaves both husband and wife (especially the former) least likely to report declining permanence, the effects of upward mobility on husband's and wife's happiness is in the opposite direction. For husbands, and even more markedly so for wives, upward mobility leads to greater likelihood of declining happiness than does downward mobility. Upward mobility seems, in other words, to make considerations of separation and/or divorce less likely but it does not guarantee the continued happiness of husband and wife.

Speculating on why this should occur, it would seem reasonable to assume, as suggested at the outset of this chapter, that movement into high status occupations--i.e., upward mobility--carries with it more social responsibility and increasing pressure to maintain respectability. These consequences of mobility upward in the status hierarchy militate against consideration of such public display of marital discord as separation or divorce proceedings. But, increased sensitivity to marital dissolution does not necessarily mean that husbands and wives in high status positions are, therefore, less likely to have difficulties with marital relationships, e.g., to have some amount of role conflict and disharmony, and to become less happy with marriage over time. As we shall see later, it may well be the case that, even though status and divorce are inversely related, husband-wife unhappiness may be directly related to status--or at least to changes in status of an upward nature.

In any event, in spite of the fact that several suggestive patterns emerge when we consider the effects of traditional measures of mobility on the husband-wife relationship, the overall conclusion must be that these measures of mobility provide very little support for the argument that occupational mobility has very large effects on the course of marital relationships. Intragenerational mobility tends to have somewhat greater an impact than does intergenerational mobility but, all in all, the results are either quite small differences or mixed effects; little or no consistency is to be found.

That the traditional measures of mobility do not seem to have very great influence on the changes in the couples' relationships should, in retrospect at least, not be too startling. At the risk of being repetitious, the context within which our couples were mobile (either upwardly or downwardly) is quite deviant from that of most samples. The occupational mobility we have been dealing with has taken place almost entirely within the confines of the middle class: the parents of these couples were, by and large, middle class and in only a very few cases did husbands and wives fall below middle class status. In other words, these couples were not newcomers to middle class status and thus, did not go through the dislocations of values and expectations that the nouveaux would be likely to undergo. At least, to modify the above slightly, measuring movement in terms of categories of occupations--e.g., professionals, managers, clerical-sales--may not adequately reflect fundamental changes in the life style of individuals who were, themselves, reared in families enjoying relatively high status.

This line of reasoning is highlighted when we investigate the possibility of an effect deriving from husband-wife differences in terms of parents' occupational status.[8] Dividing our sample into three groups--husband's parents of higher status than wife's, husband's and wife's parents of the same status, and wife's of higher status than husband's--we observed virtually no differences in terms of changes in the four indices of the marital relationship we are concerned with. While there are differences between husband's and wife's parents' status in many cases, the differences are not great--few, as we noted in Chapter One, involve spouses crossing the white collar-blue collar line. This basic homogeneity in backgrounds and the essentially middle class context of mobility serves to minimize the effects of mobility when mobility is conceptualized in terms of the usual gross occupational categories.

The theoretical importance of occupational mobility inheres in the notion that shifts in occupational status involve alterations in attitudes and behavior, and these alterations have been found to be socially disruptive. While we have not found this to be the case with our couples, using occupational movement as a measure of mobility, the basic idea--that changes in occupation lead to changes in other realms of activity--warrants further investigation. However, due to the homogeneity in status just noted, it is clear that we will have to de-emphasize this component of occupations, at least for the moment. In doing so, we come to a more direct focus on occupational _roles_ and the effects that changes in these roles have on changes in the husband-wife relationship.

Changes in Occupational Roles and Change in the Husband-Wife Relationship

Compared to the amount of work done on assessing the impact of mobility on social relationships, very little research has been conducted on the relationship between occupational roles and social relations, especially as these latter include marital relationships.[9] At the conceptual level, however, there has been much speculation on the interaction between occupational role and familial roles. Most notable in this regard has been the work of Talcott Parsons. Parsons begins his analysis by pointing out that the industrial revolution brought with it the increasing differentiation of occupational and familial structures, most clearly evidenced in the family ceasing to be a unit of economic production.[10] Intimately involved in this process of structural differentiation has been a divergence of values characterizing each of the two structures involved. On the one hand, the family has come to specialize in the sustaining of affectivity, cooperation and love and this in turn promotes individual orientations that embody this affectivity. In short, the family has become "companionate," needing love, understanding and sharing between spouses if it is to survive.[11] While the family structure has remained based on "irrational" and emotional forces, the occupational structure has gone in quite the opposite direction. Under conditions of industrialization, the occupational structure becomes increasingly rationalized and competitive. And individuals who expect to participate in the occupational structure are expected to be competitive, unemotional and impartial. In very obvious ways, then, the demands of these two structures, family and occupation, are in opposition to one another.[12] This opposition would create little friction if we were concerned only with institutional arrangements; but institutions are ultimately people engaging in social relationships and it is in these relationships that the opposition plays a potentially important part.

Familial and occupational roles overlap and family members, especially the husband, have to participate in both if the family is to survive. In doing so, family members face the necessity of essentially living two lives--one occupational and the other familial. Being full of loving kindness will not assist one greatly in the occupational world and being aggressive and competitive in the home is not the best way to get along there. Failure to keep familial and occupational roles distinct from one another can lead to conflict on one or both of the two levels. First, conflict can be located in the individual who participates in both spheres of activity--usually the husband. Some of the consequences and resolutions of this internal role conflict have been examined by Goode.[13] Conflict can also be possible at the level of interaction, interaction between two individuals, each with a differing set of role expectations.

Given the assumed fact that occupational roles and familial roles require of their incumbents differing sets of orientations to action, we are then led to suspect that any marked change in occupational role should ramify to the family role structure and, consequently, to the levels of gratification of husband and wife. This would occur, presumably, as a result of the upset in the preexisting balance worked out between the two sets of conflicting roles. One measure of change in occupational roles that is more specific than the broad occupational categories discussed above is change in type of occupation--i.e., movement between risk and nonrisk occupations. The calculability of rewards and the stability of expectations characterizing the nonrisk type of occupation should result in quite different balances between occupational and familial roles than those obtained in risk types of occupations. Movement from one type to another, therefore, should create adjustment problems for the individuals making these changes and they should then be manifest in disturbances in husband-wife relationships. What is the effect of movement between types of occupations?

Consistent with our line of reasoning, intergenerational shifts in type of occupation appear to have a rather consistent and negative effect on changes in the husband-wife relationship (see Table 4-3).[14]

Table 4-3.--FATHER'S AND SON'S TYPE OF OCCUPATION AND CHANGES IN INDICES OF HUSBAND-WIFE RELATIONSHIP

Father's and son's type of occupation	Dominance Percent of couples, both H and W increase	Consensus Percent decreasing		Happiness Percent decreasing		Permanence Percent decreasing		Number of cases
		Husband	Wife	Husband	Wife	Husband	Wife	
Same..............	23.6	52.6	60.5	41.2	44.9	36.1	38.4	215
Different..........	29.2	63.0	53.3	56.2	57.6	39.4	41.6	135

All changes, save one to be discussed in a moment, are in the predicted direction--i.e., greater likelihood of negative changes when a shift in occupational roles has occurred. Although, in some cases, the differences are slight, the consistency merits consideration.

The one exception to the general tendency of changes in type of occupation to result in negative changes in the marital relationship of husband and wife is with wife's consensus. When husband and husband's father hold different types of occupations, husband's consensus is less likely to decline. Why? Burgess and Wallin, in their initial study of adjustment in early marriage, discovered that it was the wife who generally had to make the greatest adjustment to marriage.[15] We have seen, carrying this one step further, that it is the wife who is also more likely to continue to change after the early marriage period (more wives than husbands, e.g., decreased in adjustment, consensus and happiness). Given this, and adding the assumption, consistent with the data in Table 4-3, that when the husband does not change from his father's type of occupation, he has less adjusting to do, it stands to reason that when the husband has to make little or no change, the wife will be making most if not all the changes and adjustments to new situations. Under these circumstances, it is understandable that only the wife would perceive increasing amounts of disagreement with her husband. By contrast, when the husband, by virtue of an alteration in occupational roles, also has to make some changes, there is more likely to be a "meeting halfway," with the husband now perceiving less agreement. Thus, what is functional for the husband's perceptions of consensus does not seem especially functional for the wife's. Although changes in husband's occupational role operate differently for husband's and wife's consensus, the apparent contradiction does not invalidate our line of reasoning.

This interpretation is further supported when we look at the intergenerational changes in type of occupation of both husband and wife. Wives are most likely to decline in consensus when their husbands have made no occupational change but the wife has--i.e., where the wife's father's type of occupation is different from that of her husband's. In this case, 74 percent of the wives decrease in consensus--it appears as if they do most of the giving and little of the taking. When both husband and wife make no change in type of occupation,

66 percent of the wives decrease in consensus. And where the wife has made no change but the husband has, a circumstance where the burden of change is thrust more in the husband's direction, only 56 percent of the wives decrease in consensus. With the husband, the situation most likely to produce declining consensus is, as we would expect, where the wife has made no change but the husband has. This is just the opposite of the wife's usual situation.

In rather more substantial terms, we have begun to see that the underlying logic of the mobility thesis merits some attention and certainly more attention than would be dictated solely by the effects of occupational mobility as it is normally conceived of. We have also begun to see that changes in the husband-wife relationship are not to be understood only in terms of variables intrinsic to that relationship. Rather, it now is becoming more obvious that changes in the husband-wife relationship bear some relationship to the changes that husband and wife make vis-a-vis the external environment within which the couple lives. In this "external environment," occupational roles are of central importance. Demanding of their holders a set of orientations that are quite contrary to those orientations demanded by familial roles, changes in occupational roles upset the balance that the individual maintains between occupational and familial roles and lead to increased difficulty in the marital relationship.

At this point a word of caution should be given. The data we have thus far presented only give us slight evidence for holding that occupational roles and familial roles are related. In addition, we were unable to find any relationship between specific changes in occupational role and changes in the husband-wife relationship. That is, from the data we have, it does not appear that husbands moving from risk to nonrisk occupations suffer any more dislocation than those moving from nonrisk to risk occupations. The only important thing is change.

Finding evidence supporting the basic logic of the mobility thesis--that changes in one's relationship to the occupational structure lead to changes in other relationships--leads us to consider mobility and occupational roles in greater detail. In Chapter Three, we noted that an aspect of the mobility that our couples had experienced was the fact that large numbers of husbands had greatly increased their incomes during the course of the study. For one reason or another, change in income is seldom used as a measure of mobility and yet, we think, this is by far the most widely used popular criterion in assessing an individual's success. The query "If you're so darned smart, why aren't you rich?" contains, among other things, the notion that, brains (and prestige and status) notwithstanding, money is success for most people.

Income derives from the performance of occupational roles and, presumably, the better the performance of these roles, the more income one receives. In this sense, changes in income not only represent one aspect of an individual's mobility in the society but, also, changes in income are related to the amount of time, energy and talent one invests in an occupational pursuit. It seems reasonable to assume, at any rate, that the greater one's income becomes, the more he has had to work for it; the more committed to and involved in an occupational role, the more likely the individual is to be successful in it and thereby be rewarded more highly. Changes in income, then, should be a rather sensitive indicator of both mobility and of changes in the individual's relationship to his occupational role. As such, it would also seem likely that changes in income and all that this implies should have an effect on changes in the way husband and wife relate to one another--if, of course, occupational roles are indeed related to familial roles.

Table 4-4. --CHANGE IN HUSBAND'S INCOME AND CHANGES IN INDICES OF HUSBAND-WIFE RELATIONSHIP

Change in husband's income	Dominance Percent of couples, both H and W increase	Consensus Percent decreasing		Happiness Percent decreasing		Permanence Percent decreasing		Number of cases
		Husband	Wife	Husband	Wife	Husband	Wife	
Decreased.........	15.4	57.7	30.8	23.1	30.8	26.9	38.5	26
Stable............	24.0	58.6	57.7	50.3	51.0	37.6	40.2	194
Moderate increase.	34.6	55.4	61.5	49.5	50.0	37.5	42.3	104
High increase.....	26.1	53.6	63.8	50.7	59.4	33.3	46.4	69

Table 4-4 contains the data relevant to the preceding discussion and even a cursory glance at the data contained therein indicates that changes in income are rather consistently and uniformly related to changes in the husband-wife relationship. Before we examine the substance of the findings contained in Table 4-4, let us make perfectly clear what change in income represents. We are not dealing, here, with absolute levels of income but, rather, with the degree to which income changed from one time to another. This is an extremely important point for, recalling that our measure of change is simply the middle years income divided by the early years income, we can see that if, for example, a husband started out making $12,000 a year and subsequently increased his income to $24,000 per year, by our measure his income only doubled. And with the changes in purchasing power, he was, roughly, only able to maintain his style of life. Chances are, his investment in his occupation did not increase very much. By contrast, a person who starts out with an income of $6,000 per year and increases it to $24,000 has made for himself rather significant changes in style of life and, we argue, to do so he must have greatly reallocated his energies in favor of occupational pursuits to effect such a change. In both cases, the final income is the same--but the paths by which each man got to this level of earnings are quite different. The data in Table 4-4 suggest that the paths involving strong thrusts upward--whatever the starting and finishing points--are, indeed, dangerous ones, not infrequently causing deterioration of the husband-wife relationship. The paths, however, are not uniformly problematic and do not always result in a linear progression of difficulties; let us investigate the substantive variations and their implications for the husband-wife relationship.

Looking first at changes in husband-wife authority relations, we find that the husbands least successful at increasing incomes are also the least likely to have a competitive authority relationship with their wives. Competition for dominance increases as the husbands get more successful but the most successful reverse this trend. Similar to the pattern discussed earlier (see Table 4-2), what occurs in the most successful cases is husband hegemony--in the face of a very industrious husband, the wife accedes. (Of husbands who suffered income declines, 35 percent increased in dominance; 60 percent of the most successful husbands increased in dominance). Blood and Wolfe, in their Detroit study, also noted a tendency for the very successful husband to "rule the roost."[16] Why should this be so?

Blood and Wolfe, in discussing this phenomenon, have suggested that successful husbands are competent husbands, good managers as it were, who "naturally" are able to run things better than the wife.[17] In other words, at least some skills are transferable from occupation to family. There may, however, be a less harmonious explanation for the dominance of the successful husband, In order to increase one's income sixfold or more in the space of fifteen to twenty years, it would seem that one would need to be more than a little aggressive and accustomed to having one's own way. Whether or not their business acumen carries over to being able to budget for a household is simply irrelevant: being listened to and making critical decisions during working hours is very likely to carry over into family relationships. Competent or no, the husband makes the decisions. The wife, apparently, gives in to this--but when we examine her changes in consensus, happiness and permanence, it becomes clear that, as we suggested earlier, she does so only grudgingly and is none the happier for it. It is also clear that the successful husband's hegemony does not appear to pay off for him either. An examination of the changes in consensus will begin to make clearer why we think the "pay off" does not obtain.

Husband's and wife's consensus are differently affected by changes in husband's income, a finding that is not new to us. As the husband's income increases, the wife's consensus is more likely to decrease while increases in income have a very slight tendency to reduce the husband's likelihood of decreasing in consensus. In light of our previous comments, this peculiarity is not entirely unanticipated. One of the important familial roles of the husband (if not the most important) is that of providing financial resources. As he performs this role with increasing success, and in the process gains increased hegemony, he should perceive less disagreement--as far as he is concerned, things are going quite well. Unfortunately, his wife does not appear to be nearly as content with the situation.

One very obvious reason for the wife's failure to be as content and in agreement with her husband as he becomes more and more successful may lie in the possibility that she does not share her husband's way of looking at things. In Chapter Two, we suggested that the changes in dominance and consensus indicated that husbands and wives were departing from the equalitarian and companionate relationship that typified their marriages in the early years. What seemed to be the emergent characteristic pattern of husband-wife relationship was one in which the division of labor and of authority was increasing and sharing was decreasing. Husband and wife, in other words, were moving apart and, as a result, their perceptions of consensus were being revised downwards. The data in Table 4-4 are clearly consistent with this interpretation and allow us to pursue this line of reasoning further.

Being primarily concerned with looking after children and keeping house, the wife, it would seem, comes to hold a set of criteria different from those of her husband's for evaluating the conduct of family members. She comes to expect nurturance, cooperation and love. But the husband, in order to succeed, has had to play down these responses in favor of cultivating competitiveness and "hard headedness." This divergence should be maximized when the husband has thrown himself very heavily into his occupational role--and it is here that the wife's consensus can be seen to decline most frequently. With the increasing mobility of the husband and the concomitant increased involvement in occupational roles, husband and wife come to hold divergent expectations of one another's behavior with the wife being clearly left a dissenter.[18] In other words, what we are suggesting here is that the very successful husbands are unable to leave their occupationally oriented behavior in the offices and, in bringing these orientations home with them, they create disruptions in the couple's functioning.[19]

This divergence of values has been noted by Seeley, et al., in their study of a suburban community of very successful businessmen and their families. Husbands, they report, stress competition and realism; wives stress cooperation and idealism.[20] In other words, husbands come to reflect occupational values and norms for behavior and wives come to represent the opposite and this in turn reflects the more general differentiation of husband and wife roles. It is important to recognize, however, that this is not a universal phenomenon. In couples where the husband has not been successful--where he has experienced a decline in income--his wife is least likely to report decreasing consensus and husband and wife are least likely to compete for dominance. The division of lavor and the consequent divergence of husband-wife values are, this is to say, dependent upon the husband's experiences in and relationships to the occupational structure.

Husbands are not alone, as we have seen in Chapter Three, in holding occupational roles. Many wives, at one time or another, have also held jobs and have contributed to the material well being of the family. What is the result of the wife's participation in the occupational structure? If our argument is correct, we would expect that in those couples in which the wife, too, has been employed, her roles vis-a-vis her husband's should be less clearly differentiated and her values should also be less likely to diverge from her husband's. That is, husbands and wives, when the wife has worked, should continue to share household activities and hold common expectations, thus, being less likely to decline in consensus. As the following table makes clear, this does in fact appear to be the case (see Table 4-5). While the wife's working has only a moderate effect on the husband's perception of consensus, the effect on wife's consensus is marked: her consensus is much less likely to decline when she has worked. Progressive levels of husband's success still adversely affect the wife's consensus but the relationship between consensus and wife working remains clear at each level of income increase.[21]

Table 4-5.--HUSBAND'S CHANGE IN INCOME, WIFE WORKING AND CHANGE IN HUSBAND-WIFE CONSENSUS

Change in husband's income; wife working	Change in consensus		Number of cases
	Percent husband decrease	Percent wife decrease	
Decreased			
Never worked	...	...	2
Has worked	58.3	33.3	24
Stable			
Never worked	67.9	71.4	28
Has worked	59.8	57.3	165
Moderate increase			
Never worked	53.3	73.3	15
Has worked	56.8	61.4	89
High increase			
Never worked	(63.6)	(72.7)	11
Has worked	53.4	63.8	58

The logic of our line of reasoning has led us to a consideration of changes in occupational roles and the effect these changes have on husband-wife relationships. The data we have presented thus far indicate that changes in occupational roles do affect marital relationships and they do so in a rather specific way. By taking success as one aspect of occupational role change, we have seen that the greater the success--i.e., the more the husband has increased his income over time--the greater the growing apart of husband and wife. However, it is crucial to note that the sharpest difference occurs between the couples in which the husband's income has declined and those couples in which the husband's income remained stable. From this latter point on, greater increments in income add only slightly to the likelihood of negative changes in the husband-wife relationship.

The normal course of affairs in the middle class is, of course, to at least keep pace with the cost of living and, hopefully, work hard enough to keep income rising at a pace faster than the cost of living. To the extent that this normal expectation requires relatively high levels of involvement in occupational pursuits on the part of the husband, it may well be that, as a consequence, the differentiation of husband-wife activities is also typical: typical but unsatisfying. Blood and Wolfe, for example, have noted the tendency for the wives of "busy businessmen" to be less satisfied than other wives.[22] When looked at over time, this phenomenon appears to extend well beyond wives of "busy businessmen." The point is that it seems that only in instances where the husband has been so lacking in interest--or whatever it takes to garner ever larger salaries year after year--do we find that the marital relationship is more likely to improve than not. It is essential to point out here that the husbands whose incomes declined are not failures in the ordinary sense of the word. They still have white collar jobs, nearly half being either a professional or manager, and, in terms of their parents' status, they have moved above the occupational levels of their parents. If we were dealing with out and out failures--men "on the skids"--things would no doubt be quite different. As it is, the most reasonable conclusion seems to be simply that these men are simply more interested in their families than in their occupations and, as a result, on virtually every count, the husbands and wives in these couples are better off--maritally, not financially. In sum, the most significant difference is not between the most successful and all others, but, rather, between the least successful and all others.

It should also be clear that it is not success itself that creates the problems we have seen; it is what is demanded of husbands in the process of becoming successful. They are required to spend more and more time and energy at and in work. This leaves less time and energy to be spent around the house. The consequence is a shift in the bases of the husband-wife relationship, a shift that involves moving from a joint role relationship to a more segregated role relationship. Husband and wife grow apart and, in the process, conflict more with one another and become less happy with and confident about their marriage. When, however, the wife also assumes an occupation role at one or another point in the marriage, the likelihood of this growing apart is lessened. This, we suggest is the result of the fact that husband-wife activities in couples where the wife works are less likely to be highly differentiated--the husband is more likely to help out with housework and children and husband-wife values are less likely to diverge.

The interpretation we have been developing here rests upon the assumption that occupational role performance demands, if one is to be successful, values and behavior contradictory to the continued successful performance of familial roles. We have seen earlier that intergenerational change in the type of occupational roles pursued creates disturbances in the husband's ability to reach a satisfactory balance between occupational roles and familial roles. We have just seen and been discussing the fact that changes in the husband's occupational role performance, in the course of his own career, also exact their price in the form of increased husband-wife conflict and decreased husband-wife gratification with marriage. The combination of these two propositions should, logically at least, allow us to specify even further the relationship between occupational roles and familial roles and how changes in one relate to changes in the other.

We would expect that under conditions where the husband has made a break with the occupational type of his father and, at the same time, has been highly successful in his own right, his occupational role performance should interfere most markedly with his and his wife's ability to sustain a consensual, mutually gratifying relationship. By contrast, where the husband has maintained occupational continuity with his father and not been especially successful, husband and wife should be least likely to find themselves reporting greater conflict with one another and consequent reductions in levels of gratification. This, as Table 4-6 clearly demonstrates, is the case.[23]

In successive stages of analysis, we have moved closer to a specification of the relationship between changes in occupational roles and changes in the husband-wife relationship. We have discovered that changes in occupational roles that involve 1) marked breaks with one's past experiences and/or 2) increased involvement in an occupational milieu, are most likely to result in increased husband-wife conflict and decreased gratification. This is essentially the result

Table 4-6.--CHANGE IN HUSBAND'S INCOME AND TYPE OF OCCUPATION, AND CHANGE IN INDICES OF HUSBAND-WIFE RELATIONSHIP

Changes in income and type of occupation	Dominance Percent of couples, both H and W increase	Consensus Percent decreasing		Happiness Percent decreasing		Permanence Percent decreasing		Number of cases
		Husband	Wife	Husband	Wife	Husband	Wife	
Decrease								
Same	15.8	57.9	36.8	10.5	26.3	26.3	42.1	19
Different	...	...	...	...	...	...	...	5
Stable								
Same	16.0	56.8	56.7	44.7	48.9	37.2	37.2	94
Different	31.5	63.0	50.7	53.4	52.0	41.1	41.1	73
Moderate increase								
Same	36.4	52.7	61.8	43.4	39.6	39.6	35.8	55
Different	31.4	54.3	60.0	57.1	60.0	31.4	42.9	35
High increase								
Same	26.7	53.5	74.4	44.4	53.3	33.3	44.4	45
Different	23.8	76.2	61.9	61.9	71.4	47.6	42.9	21

of the increases in familial role specialization accompanying these kinds of activities, sharing less, communicating less and, thus, agreeing less with one another's conceptions of how the family should be run. A reduction in happiness and permanence also flows from this situation. However, when the wife also participates in the occupational structure, we find the likelihood of these negative changes taking place reduced significantly. This, we think, is due to the reduction in husband-wife role differentiation. In situations where both husband and wife work--their values are more likely to be similar and remain that way and their activities are, almost by definition, less distinct from one another.

The individual's occupation and, more importantly, his relationship to that occupation, while obviously of extreme importance, is only one of the many points of contact the individual has (or can have) with the broader social networks comprising his milieu. We would like now to examine the interaction of changes in husband-wife activity in the community with the dynamics of their relationship to one another. We will then turn, by way of summarizing our analysis, to a consideration of the combined effects of changes in occupational role and changes in community activity on changes in the husband-wife relationship.

Community Activity and Changes in the Marital Relationship

Community activity has typically been viewed as threatening to the husband-wife bond. Time spent at meetings is time spent away from home. Implicit in this view is a particular image of the modern community and the organizations it supports. Burgess has argued that the community of a century ago, small, placid and tightly integrated, actually bolstered the husband-wife bond.[24] Participation in the life of the community was, for all intents and purposes, simply an extension of family relationships and, what with a high degree of value consensus in the community, such participation simply reaffirmed one's commitment to the marital relationship. As the city grew, as it became the center of industry, value consensus began to disintegrate and people began to interact with one another segmentally--i. e., rationally and without emotion. Under these circumstances, involvement in the community came to be disruptive of family interests and values. Indeed, the city now posed alternative attractions to family members. Movies, clubs, dances, nightclubs--all competed for the family member's attention. Long before the term "mass society" came of vogue, the Chicago School was using this notion to explain the rising rates of social and personal disorganization, with marital instability foremost among the signs of this instability. For the married person, participation in the modern community--more aptly, the metropolis--no longer reaffirms values of family stability.

While there is no question that communities and hence community participation have been altered with increases in size and complexity of communities, it is, we think, less than clear that the changes have been necessarily inimical to family stability. Belonging to many organizations, although this certainly precludes extended hours spent with family members gathered around the hearth reading stories and singing together, may increase the social costs of disrupting the marital bond. Inhibiting divorce, of course, is not the same thing as promoting satisfied husbands and wives. Doubtlessly, no satisfied couples get divorced but this has not yet come to mean that all dissatisfied couples do get divorced. How then does change in community activity affect change in the husband-wife relationship? Does increasing community activity result in decreasing commitment to one's marriage or does increasing involvement bolster the unity of the husband-wife bond?

Before we begin to attempt to answer these and related questions, we should reiterate the fact that our data on these matters are something less than comprehensive. For example, as we pointed out in Chapter Three, we have no knowledge of actual participation in community organizations. All we know are the numbers of organizations each spouse belonged and belongs to. It is also peculiar that in a schedule designed by Burgess the question of joint husband-wife participation in organizations was only very obliquely asked and, for all practical purposes, we have no information on whether or not, in joining (or dropping) organizational memberships, husbands and wives were joining the same organizations. This poses a grave problem since we would suspect, a priori, that husband and wife joining the same organizations is quite different a thing than their joining different organizations. In both cases, spouses could be joining the same number of organizations: we have only the numbers. In addition, studies have shown that much depends upon the type of organizations belonged to--some organizations or forms of participation seem to be supportive of the husband-wife relationship and others seem to be quite divisive.[25] These types of omissions in our information will necessarily make our comments conditional. But enough of what we do not have; let us see what information we can glean from the data we do have.

One community organization that is clearly supportive of marital bonds, in doctrine at any rate, is the church. We noted earlier that interfaith marriages are typically less likely to succeed than are marriages between members of the same faith. This is partly the result of husband-wife disagreements over religion (and especially the religious training of children) which can add an element of divisiveness to the marriage. Also, however, homogamy in terms of religion generally means joint husband-wife participation in church activities (at least worship), thereby reinforcing their commitments to one another. Religious intermarriage, for our couples, does not seem to count for much. This can be seen clearly in terms of changes in husband's and wife's considerations of separation and/or divorce (permanence). Intermarried couples are only slightly more likely to have decreased in permanence (see Table 4-7). The data in Table

Table 4-7.--RELIGION OF SPOUSES AND PERCENTAGE DECREASING IN PERMANENCE

Spouse's religion	Percent decreasing in permanence		Number of cases
	Husband	Wife	
Both same..........	36.9	39.5	301
Protestant.......	34.6	38.5	182
Catholic.........	42.9	42.9	21
Jew..............	36.2	38.8	80
None.............	55.6	50.0	18
Husband and wife different.........	40.8	47.9	71

4-7 reveal that intermarriage is not so bad as long as spouses maintain at least a nominal tie to a religious doctrine. Those couples in which no religious identification is expressed are the most likely to have given thought to dissolving marriage. With the exception of the irreligious, however, nominal identification with a religious body makes very little difference in terms of the course of change in husband-wife relationships.

If nominal identification has relatively little bearing on changes in the husband-wife relationship, perhaps changes in their actual church attendance will have some effect. Only in the case of changes in permanence do we find changes in church attendance having any effect and the effect is in a quite predictable direction: increased attendance lessens the likelihood of contemplating the dissolution of one's marriage; "backsliding" yields increased likelihood of contemplation of divorce or separation.[26] However, church attendance has little or no effect on husband-wife happiness. In other words, as a distinctive community organization, participation in church services has little influence on the abilities of husband and wife to continue to get along with one another but it does have sufficient influence on the attitudes of husband and wife to dampen their willingness to consider severing their marriage vows.

As with changes in church participation, changes in husband-wife general activity in community organizations has relatively little effect on the changes in their relationship to one another (see Table 4-8). With few exceptions, couples in which both husband and wife

Table 4-8.--CHANGE IN HUSBAND-WIFE ORGANIZATIONAL ACTIVITY AND CHANGE IN HUSBAND-WIFE RELATIONSHIP

Husband-wife organizational activity	Dominance Percent of couples, both H and W increase	Consensus Percent decreasing		Happiness Percent decreasing		Permanence Percent decreasing		Number of cases
		Husband	Wife	Husband	Wife	Husband	Wife	
Both increase	26.3	57.5	62.2	48.9	53.7	33.5	41.0	188
Husband increase, wife decrease	20.6	47.6	58.7	54.0	52.4	34.9	41.3	63
Wife increase, husband decrease	25.8	58.1	50.0	41.9	43.5	46.8	37.1	62
Both decrease	32.9	61.4	58.6	48.6	54.3	40.0	48.6	70

decrease their activity in the community are most likely to experience declines in all aspects of their marital relationship. The opposite circumstance, where both increase their activity, is not, however, most integrative for the husband-wife union. It is important to stress both sides of the coin here because if the relationship was symmetrical--i.e., if husband-wife withdrawal from the community was related to increased husband-wife difficulty and increased involvement in the community was related to better husband-wife relationships--we would be led to suggest that perhaps changes in husband-wife relationships resulted in changes in community involvement and not the other way around. This, of course, is still a possibility but support for holding that the causal relationship flows from the family to activities and not the other way around is not very strong. In short, there seems to be no consistent relationship of any great strength between changes in the patterns of husband-wife involvement in community organizations, including religious organizations, and changes in their marital relationship.

Before discounting the efficacy of this aspect of the lives of our couples, let us recall that at the close of Chapter Three we noted a rather interesting relationship between changes in the husband's income and changes in the organizational behavior of husband and wife: as income increased by ever larger jumps, husband and wife increased their memberships in organizations, except in the situation where the husband's income had taken an extremely large jump between the early and middle years of marriage. In this case, the likelihood of his joining more organizations dropped off precipitously. Although changes in organizational activity obviously has little independent effect on changes in marriage, perhaps when we consider changes in organizational activity and changes in occupational success simultaneously, we will be able to discern a clearer picture. Let us consider this for a moment.

We have seen earlier in this chapter that the greater the increase in husband's income, the greater the likelihood of husband-wife role dislocations--movement away from an equalitarian role relationship and, concomitantly, increased husband-wife conflict over the performance of familial roles--and the greater the likelihood of losses in happiness and permanence. The difficulty in role relationships was felt most heavily by the wife but, in terms of losses in happiness and permanence, problems were equally evident with both husband and wife. The reason for this situation, as we see it, is not that "money is the root of all evil," but, rather, that in the process of making ever greater amounts of money, the husband is forced to commit himself ever more thoroughly to his occupational role. At the same time, by virtue of both nature and nurture, the wife typically comes to vastly greater commitment to specifically family roles. The result, when both of these conditions are met, is a growing apart of husband and wife. They cease having an equalitarian role relationship and they are less happy with and less committed to their marriage.

This being the case, it would not seem at all unreasonable to assume that changes in other commitments to structures external to the couple would also have a bearing on the situation. Table 4-9

Table 4-9.--CHANGE IN HUSBAND'S INCOME, CHANGE IN HUSBAND'S AND WIFE'S ORGANIZATIONAL AFFILIATIONS, AND CHANGE IN INDICES OF THE HUSBAND-WIFE RELATIONSHIP

Changes in income and organizational affiliations	Dominance Percent of couples, both H and W increase	Consensus Percent decreasing		Happiness Percent decreasing		Permanence Percent decreasing		Number of cases
		Husband	Wife	Husband	Wife	Husband	Wife	
Income decrease								
H decreases........	9.1	63.6	9.1	9.1	27.3	36.4	18.2	11
H increases........	20.0	60.0	46.7	33.3	33.3	20.0	53.3	15
High increase								
H decreases........	52.6	69.0	51.7	41.4	44.8	41.4	41.4	29
H increases........	20.0	45.0	75.0	57.5	70.0	35.0	50.0	40
Income decrease								
W decreases........	8.3	66.7	25.0	16.7	30.8	16.7	30.8	12
W increases........	21.4	57.1	35.7	28.6	28.6	35.7	42.9	14
High increase								
W decreases........	42.9	66.7	76.2	66.7	66.7	33.3	52.4	21
W increases........	15.6	48.9	63.4	42.2	57.8	40.0	44.4	45

presents a summary of the data relating change in husband's income, change in husband's and wife's organizational activity and changes in the husband-wife marital relationship. We have presented only the extremes of change in husband's income only for the sake of simplicity--the addition of the other two strata (husband's income stable and moderately increased) do not change the patterns at all. Also, for want of sufficient cases, we are unable to treat husband's and wife's organizational activity together. This will not, we think, interfere greatly with our analysis. What are the results of this combination of changes in income and changes in organizational activity and what light do they shed on our interpretation?

There are two ways of approaching this question, each of which gives a slightly different but complementary view of the changes experienced by these couples. The first of these approaches is simply to examine the effects of change in organizational activity at each income level. The second is to treat changes in income and changes in organizational activity as of one piece--as changes in external commitments--and observe how various degrees of change in external commitments affect changes in marriage. We will examine each of these. Looking first at the effects of changes in husband's organizational activity, we find that when income is taken into account, these changes definitely do have an impact on the course of change in the husband-wife relationship: increases in the husband's organizational activity generally result in rather striking reductions in the quality of the marital relationship. There are, of course, exceptions to this general tendency. First of all, increased organizational activity seems to reduce the husband's willingness to give serious consideration to divorce and/or separation. This is somewhat ironic since the wives of these men do not seem likely to have given their husbands cause for optimism--when the husbands increase activity, wives are much more likely to report declines in consensus, happiness and permanence. Husbands, too, are more likely to report declines in happiness when their organizational activity increases, regardless of change in income. This suggests that perhaps the husband's consideration of divorce and/or separation is contingent more upon external factors, e.g., friends and associates, than upon his or his spouse's evaluations of the state of their marriage.

The other exception to the general pattern is by now a familiar companion: husband's and wife's evaluations of their role relationship vary from one another's. Especially for those whose incomes have been greatly enlarged, what promotes the husband's sense of consensus does the opposite for the wife. The critical point to note is that when the husband's income has decreased but he has increased his external involvements in other ways, husband and wife compete for dominance more than when he reduces other external commitments. But, the very successful husbands find things just reversed--at least as far as the husband is concerned. He assumes dominance and few wives challenge his hegemony. His perceptions of agreement with his wife are thereby augmented in spite of the fact that, as far as his wife is concerned, things have changed for the worse.

In order to make sense out of both the major pattern and the deviations from it that we have just discussed, we need to examine the situation in a more general perspective. For the husband, changes in income and changes in organizational activity clearly represent changes in the overall extent to which he is either committed to the external structures of the community or to his relationship to his wife and family. When he is relatively aloof from his occupation, when for example, his income has declined, and he has also withdrawn from organizations, we can assume that his focus of activity is rather highly confined to his family. By contrast, heavy involvement in occupational pursuits, such that income increases by leaps and bounds, coupled with stepped up organizational activity should leave little time and energy for specifically family directed activities. Looking at marriages in this perspective, we find that almost without exception husbands heavily committed to extra-familial activities (including occupational) are more likely to find themselves in deteriorating marital situations than are husbands least committed to extra-familial activities. Under conditions of maximum external commitment, it is not hard to envision a rather thoroughly organized family--certain tasks, principally focused around outside responsibilities, for the husband and another, completely distinct set of tasks, focused on the home, for the wife. While this arrangement is most favorable for the husband's perception of consensus--perhaps only because he is rather insulated from and unaware of the actual workings of the family; it is in this type of situation that husband and wife alike are the most likely to become less happy with marriage. In short, as the press of extra-familial activities increases on the husband, husband and wife, and especially the wife, tend to grow apart, do different things and, thus, experience declining gratification from the marital relationship.

We saw earlier when we examined the effect of the wife's working that it was a mistake to ignore her extra-familial activities. When we turn to a consideration of how changes in her organizational affiliations modify the above situation, we find several interesting things occurring. For the wives of husbands who have failed to garner increased monetary rewards from the occupational world, changes in organizational activity closely parallel, in terms of their effects, those of her husband's: increased organizational activity is disadvantageous to the husband-wife relationship. It seems reasonable to assume that the wives who increase their external commitments under these circumstances do so as a means of compensating for the felt failures of the husband in the occupational world. At any rate, whatever the motivations involved, increased activity on the part of the wife does nothing to help the marriage along. When we look at the effects of changes in the activity of the wives of the very successful husbands, however, a rather sharp reversal in the effect of increased activity takes place. Here we find that increased extra-familial activity of wives is less disruptive than decreased activity. (As with husband's activity, though, the increased activity of the wives of successful husbands is still more disruptive than decreased activity of the wives of unsuccessful husbands--we will return to this.) Why should this be so?

Recalling our sketch of the husband-wife relationship in couples where the husband is "on the go," it seems clear that where the wife cuts down on her outside activities, the separation of husband's from wife's activities would be at a maximum--the husband is heavily committed to job and organizations and the wife becomes almost exclusively a homemaker. Dissension, unhappiness and thoughts of dissolving the marriage abound. In no other group of couples do we find a greater likelihood of husband and wife decreasing in consensus and happiness. Under these circumstances, husband and wife are very likely to come into conflict over authority. No doubt each views the other as having "unrealistic" views of how the family should be run since each is looking at the family from a different vantage point.

In contrast to this highly divisive situation, when the wife of the very successful husband takes upon herself additional external commitments in the form of increased organizational activity, conflict and unhappiness are somewhat less likely. Under these circumstances, one of two things can be operating. First, organizations may function in ways similar to the wife's working. That is, increased participation in organizations may inhibit the otherwise very great likelihood of husband's and wife's values and role images drifting apart. The wife who is given a chance to take on and sustain roles and orientations other than those restricted to the home is in somewhat better a position to understand her husband's activities and the expectations deriving from his activities. The division of labor between husband and wife is probably lessened (although not to the extent that her working would tend to retard division of labor) and they can share ideas and activities more freely and readily under these circumstances. The other alternative is considerably more pessimistic but nonetheless altogether possible, at least in some instances. This alternative can best be pointed out by reference to the adage "absence makes the heart grow fonder." Confronted with a very busy husband, if the wife too becomes heavily involved in extra-familial activities, little time is left for husband-wife interaction. In what would otherwise be a conflictful situation, the lack of communication may serve to restrain conflict--no talking, no fighting. Each being left to his own devices, there is little to have arguments over. Of course, in this rather overdrawn situation, there is also very little to be happy about insofar as we are concerned with marital happiness. Whatever the specific dynamic in these very outgoing couples, the fact remains that the wife and her husband are less likely to report a declining marital relationship when the wife assumes some of the burden of involvement in the community.

It is important, lest the reader mistakenly assume that the ideal situation is one in which the wife and the husband are maximally involved in extra-familial activities, to note that insofar as our data indicate, the fewer the external commitments of husband and wife, the more likely they are to experience increased happiness and conflict-free role relationships. There are, it would seem, limits to the extent to which withdrawal from community participation serves to augment the marital relationship. It must be borne in mind that we are not dealing here with absolutely uninvolved men and women; nor are we discussing absolute occupational failures. Rather, the distinction we are drawing is between the balancing of external and internal commitments as opposed to the extreme of over-involvement in activities and roles external and contradictory to the activities and roles necessary for stable, rewarding family life. The tipping point seems to be that point where husband and wife begin, by force of commitments, to live separate lives, each with its own distinct set of demands and rewards. Some specialization of roles is no doubt necessary and inevitable and not greatly destructive of the bases for rewarding husband-wife interaction. When specialization is markedly more progressive, however, we have found the likelihood of husband and wife finding continued ease in relating to one another strikingly diminished.

FOOTNOTES

1. William J. Goode, Women in Divorce (originally published as After Divorce) (New York: The Free Press of Glencoe, 1956), Chapter Four.

2. No attempt will be made here to summarize the vast literature on this topic. For a short but thorough review, see Joseph A. Kahl, The American Class Structure (New York: Rinehart and Co., 1960).

3. Burgess and Cottrell, op. cit., pp. 121-32; Julius Roth and Robert F. Peck, "Social Class and Social Mobility Factors Related to Marital Adjustment," in Robert F. Winch and Robert McGinnis (eds.), Selected Studies in Marriage and the Family (New York: Holt, 1953), pp. 471-85.

4. For a summary of some of this work, see William J. Goode, The Family (Englewood Cliffs, N.J.: Prentice-Hall, 1964), pp. 86-88.

5. The classic treatment of the effects of mobility is given by Pitirim Sorokin, Social and Cultural Mobility (New York: The Free Press of Glencoe, 1959), especially Chapter Twenty-two.

6. Again, we will not attempt to summarize this literature. For an extensive review of the more outstanding studies, see Bruno Bettelheim and Morris Janowitz, Social Change and Prejudice (New York: The Free Press of Glencoe, 1964), pp. 25-48.

7. Roth and Peck, op. cit., pp. 479-80.

8. Roth and Peck report evidence that cross-class marriages are less well adjusted than same-class marriages. Ibid., pp. 475-76.

9. There have been numerous studies on the sub-cultures of various esoteric occupational groups--e.g., jazz musicians. Little or nothing has been done for more common occupational pursuits. Cf. Harold L. Wilensky, op. cit.

10. Parsons and Bales, op. cit., pp. 8-10. This process is described in detail in Neil Smelser, Social Change in the Industrial Revolution (Chicago: The University of Chicago Press, 1959), pp. 180-312.

11. Ibid., pp. 16-22. The family, Parsons argues, has now the prime function of "personality maintenance"--a notion very similar to Burgess' "companionship."

12. See Talcott Parsons, "The Social Structure of the Family," in Ruth N. Anshen, (ed.), The Family: Its Function and Destiny (New York: Harper and Bros., rev. ed., 1959), p. 262; Talcott Parsons, The Social System (Glencoe, Ill.: The Free Press, 1950), pp. 176-80.

13. William J. Goode, "A Theory of Role Strain," American Sociological Review (1960), 25:483-95.

14. Contrary to our expectations, however, we found no differences between risk and nonrisk occupations or between movements from one to the other. The important factor is change, per se, not change from what to what.

15. Burgess and Wallin, op. cit., pp. 614-15.

16. Blood and Wolfe, op. cit., p. 31.

17. Ibid., pp. 29-46.

18. One of the reasons for the apparent immunity of the very successful husbands from the disagreements perceived by the wife may be a decline in communication between spouses. We do not have information on communication between spouses but Blood and Wolfe report that the wives of very successful husbands complain more frequently than others about a lack of communication. Ibid., pp. 193-95.

19. Other studies have demonstrated the fact that husbands do not appear to leave their work at 5:00 p.m. See, for example, David F. Aberle and Kaspar D. Naegele, "Middle Class Fathers' Occupational Role and Attitudes toward Children," in Norman W. Bell and Ezra F. Vogel, (ed.) The Family (Glencoe, Ill.: The Free Press, 1960), pp. 126-36.

20. John R. Seeley, R. Alexander Sim and Elizabeth W. Loosley, Crestwood Heights (New York: John Wiley and Sons, Science Editions, 1963), pp. 382-94.

21. Since it would confuse issues to present the effects of wife working on the other variables, let us briefly call the reader's attention to the fact that the same pattern holds for both happiness and permanence. Working wives are less likely than nonworking wives to have decreased in happiness and permanence. (The effect on husbands is in the same direction but much less significant.) For example, in the "high increase" cases, 82 percent of the wives who had never worked declined in happiness; 63 percent of the working wives declined.

22. Blood and Wolfe, op. cit., pp. 169-72.

23. We continue to observe the same patterns of relationship between changes in income and changes in husband-wife dominance and consensus. We see no need to repeat our earlier comments regarding this.

24. Burgess, Locke and Thomas, op. cit., Chapter Sixteen.

25. Purnell Benson, "The Interests of Happily Married Couples," Marriage and Family Living, (1952), 14:276-80.

26. The percentages involved are as follows: 48 percent of the consistent non-attenders declined in permanence; 35 percent of the consistent attenders declined; of those who began going after the early years, 30 percent declined; of those who stopped, 44 percent.

V
SOCIAL CHANGE AND THE FAMILY

Most, if not all, of the marriages we have been analyzing have undergone transformations of one kind or another during the fifteen year course of this study. For some, change represented improvement in the husband-wife relationship; for most, change involved the opposite. The predominant change can, we think, best be interpreted as an emotional "deadening" of the husband-wife relationship. Husbands and wives report declining happiness and, closely related to this, declining love for one another. Pineo, in his treatment of marital change in these same marriages, reported that the responses to three items figured centrally in this change: 1) spouses expressed many more regrets with their marriages in the middle as opposed to the early years of the study; 2) spouses had, by the middle years, strong doubts about "doing it all over again" with the same person; and 3) spouses demonstrated less affection for one another over time.[1] The last item is especially crucial since it represents a translation of thought (doubts about the wisdom of marrying one's spouse) into action (declining affective response to one's spouse). Thus it is not difficult to understand why we also found husbands' and wives' commitments to marriage declining in so large a number of cases. William Goode, in discussing several types of problem marriages, describes what he calls the "empty shell" marriage in terms that are relevant here. He writes:

> In the empty shell marriages members no longer feel any strong commitment to many of their mutual role obligations....Parents...fulfill their <u>instrumental</u> obligations, but not their expressive ones. The husband holds a job and provides for the family. The wife takes care of the house and meals and nurses those who become ill....But any spontaneous expression of affection...is rebuffed by the others. The hostility in such a home is great...[2] (emphasis in the original)

It must be stressed that we see such a condition as described by Goode as a polar or ideal type toward which many of our couples are moving: some have undoubtedly realized this situation, others are close to it, and still others (probably the majority in our sample) have quite a distance to travel and may never reach the "empty shell" condition. But the important point is that a large proportion of our couples are headed in this direction--far more than the proportion moving in the opposite direction. Moreover, and this is of special significance given the initial aims of the study's designers, Burgess and Wallin, these changes cannot be predicted from the engagement profiles or the early marriage relationships of husbands and wives. That is, the changes we have observed do not seem to be the result of peculiarities in spouses' background characteristics or of unfortunate mistakes made in the courtship of these individuals. Rather, the changes result more from what husband and wife do _after_ their marriage. The relationship between their behavior before and after marriage is not, apparently, such that a simple projection from one to the other works. This can be seen most clearly when we recall that husbands and wives, in terms of backgrounds and initial adjustments to one another in marriage, appeared to be ideally--or nearly ideally--suited to one another. What then accounts for the progressive deadening of the emotional content of these marriages?

In the first instance, our answer to this question is that the movement toward the "empty shell" type of marriage is highly related to a change in the role relationships of husband and wife. Decreasing husband-wife happiness and permanence is disproportionately common in those marriages which move toward a greater degree of role differentiation. Most of our couples began their marriages with relatively low levels of separation between husband and wife roles. Authority was rather evenly distributed between husband and wife and, as a result, decisions were made jointly. Arguments were rare and when they did occur, disagreements were settled by mutual give and take. Most wives worked to help augment the family's income and we surmise that, given these other features, husbands could be found frequently helping their wives with traditionally feminine household tasks. By the middle years, however, this reasonable undifferentiated role arrangement had undergone alterations. Authority came to be centered around one spouse or both husband and wife took on increasing dominance, competing, as it were, for authority. As a result of this change in the balance of authority, both husband and wife reported declining agreement with one another, with a concomitant increase in the frequency and severity of conflict.

As we noted in Chapter Two, others have observed the tendency for role differentiation to become more pronounced in the course of the marital relationship.[3] Parsons and Bales, on the basis of the latter's research on small group processes, have elaborated this finding and have suggested that husband-wife role differentiation serves to enhance the functioning of the family group (as role differentiation enhances the smooth, goal-directed, operation of the experimental small group).[4] In some respects this may be so. It might well be the case that the couple is rendered more efficient with an increased division of labor. However, our data directly, and others' more indirectly[5], contradict this evaluation of the effects of role differentiation. As role differentiation increases, husbands and wives in our sample are increasingly likely to argue over family decisions; they are increasingly likely to suffer losses in happiness; and, finally, they are much more likely to give increasingly serious consideration to separation and/or divorce. Increasing role differentiation does anything but enhance the husband-wife relationship.

By indirection and extrapolation, several rather recent studies also provide a basis for questioning the extent to which children are well served in a highly differentiated family. First of all, there is increasing evidence indicating that the children of working mothers are no less well adjusted than the children of mothers who remain at home. As a matter of fact, in some respects the former may be somewhat better adjusted.[6] There are several possible ways of accounting for this, but the most compelling from our point of view is to deal with socialization in terms of both husband and wife and, consequently, in terms of the husband-wife relationship. Sears, et al., have noted that the father typically enters directly into the socialization of subsequent children.[7] This is in conformity with what we would expect to be the normal pattern, given the tendency for husband-wife role differentiation to increase over time. However, in families where the wife also works, it is clear that role differentiation is retarded, with the husband assuming some of the household--i.e., specifically family--tasks. Although direct evidence on this is wanting, it seems reasonable to suggest that the father also continues to share at least some active responsibility for the socialization of all children, not just the first-born. Thus, although the child's interaction with the mother is reduced when she works, his interaction with his parents may not be greatly reduced at all. In other words, the child may have a more balanced set of relationships with his parents in cases where both mother and father work.[8]

There are at least two possible reasons for the differences in observation and interpretation between Parsons' and Bales' work and the present work. The first involves the nature of the data used in each. The family, while in some senses a small group, is not comparable to other small groups: not in composition (usually), not in duration, nor in terms of purpose. As a result, what may serve to integrate individuals who have come together (or are assembled) for the express purpose of getting something done should not necessarily be expected to do the same for individuals who are expected--and expect themselves--to interact with few specific goals in mind and for very long periods of time. One of the reasons, then, for our differences inheres in the incomparability of the family and other small groups. Parsons and Bales, we argue, were generalizing from too limited a range of phenomena.[9]

The second source of discrepancy is less methodological and more substantive, stemming from what we hold to be an overly rational characterization of the family by Parsons and Bales. In the abstract, the family can be said to perform certain functions for the larger society, as Parsons and Bales contend. At this abstract level, one can then analyze the ways in which families organize themselves for the smooth performance of these responsibilities. Division of labor--role differentiation--is undoubtedly an efficient way of organizing activities, as long as the individuals involved are more or less conscious of and in agreement with the ends to be met by this organization. As a host of observers have pointed out, among them Durkheim, Simmel and Toennies, however, interpersonal relationships are altered by changes in the division of labor. At the interpersonal level, the lowest level of abstraction, this involves the segmentalization of relationships. In the family, this may result in the better performance of the husband in his occupational role--an abstract "need" of the society's--and the (presumably) more efficient rearing of children and caring for the household by the wife. This would be integrative for the family as long as these ends, these societal "needs," are expected to be more than breadwinners and wives are expected to be more than nurse-housekeepers. In our society, at any rate, husband and wife are expected to be companions who attempt to understand one another and who share innermost feelings and activities with one another. In short, they are not expected--and the evidence indicates that they do not, themselves, expect--to have segmental relationships with one another. The outcome is clear: as husband-wife roles are increasingly differentiated, as the husband-wife relationship becomes more segmental, the emotional content of the relationship begins to lose force. Love declines, less affection is demonstrated less often, and husbands and wives are less likely to be happy with their marriages.

Intimately connected with the interrelated processes of increasing differentiation and declining gratification are the changes in husband's and wife's relationships to the external world, especially the occupational structure. Our evidence has indicated that certain changes in relationships to external social structures, more than any pressures generated internally by, say, the birth of a child, seem to result in the greater likelihood of increased differentiation and decreased gratification. That is, there seem to be few features of the husband-wife relationship, per se, that create "needs" for increased husband-wife role differentiation. The primary source of increasing husband-wife role differentiation, as far as our couples are concerned, is to be found in the occupational demands made upon the husband and his reaction to these demands.[10] With increasing success in occupational endeavors (as measured by the degree to which the husband's income increased), we found increasing role differentiation and loss of gratification.

This situation can be viewed in several different ways, the most obvious of which is simple in terms of time. There are a fixed number of hours in the day. The more of these hours that come to be devoted to occupational roles--and it seems more than reasonable to assume that the successful have had to devote more time to their jobs than have the less successful, on the average at least--the less time there is left available for the performance of specifically familial roles and activities. In order that these latter roles get performed, then, it is the wife who must do them. In spite of the ideals and values held by husband and wife, time spent in occupational pursuits is time spent away from the family, and, almost necessarily, results in increased differentiation of husband-wife roles.

While this situation is no doubt less satisfactory, especially for the wife, than a situation where time spent with the family is more or less constant (and high), it should be clear that alterations in time allocations are only one aspect of the emergence of conflict and lowered gratification that we have been observing. Another, and in some ways more fundamental, feature of this situation is simply the incompatibility of values and expectations that surround occupational and familial roles. To be very successful in occupational pursuits requires a fairly active acceptance of the modes of interpersonal interaction predominant in the occupational world. To be successful, one has to be competitive and aggressive; others have to be viewed more as means than as ends and, as a result, they tend to be judged with some degree of rationality and calculation. The family, obviously, defines the modes of interpersonal relationship differently: individuals should mildly and cheerfully cooperate with others in the family group; family members are to be loved, to be treated as ends--and not as means.

Given this polarity, differentiation of husband-wife roles along the axis of occupational-familial specializations creates dilemmas in the relationship between husband and wife. When husbands specialize in occupational activities and when wives specialize in familial activities, consensus on the fundamentals of family living should be made more problematic since each is accustomed to quite different styles of operating in respective roles. And, over time, when we observed these specializations becoming more distinct, we do in fact find that conflict increases and, as a result, levels of happiness and permanence are lowered. In other words, while there is some reason to expect that increasing differentiation, as such, is destructive of the ability of husband and wife to sustain a mutually satisfying relationship, it is especially that differentiation which requires husband and wife to hold differing expectations that is destructive of the husband-wife relationship. When, over time, circumstances that produce differentiation (e.g., success in one's occupational role) were avoided, we found that husband-wife conflict more often than not decreased over time and, similarly, husband-wife gratification was more likely to increase. In the extreme cases where these conditions that produce pressures toward differentiaiton were not avoided, the opposite occurred: increased conflict was highly probable (76 percent of the wives reported decreased consensus) and happiness and permanence were most likely to decrease.

In our analysis, we attempted to specify those conditions that produce pressures for differentiation on the couple. They were: 1) increasing success of the husband in his occupational role and 2) the withdrawal of the wife from the external world, occupational and organizational. We also noted that the reverse of these two conditions produced far fewer negative changes in the husband-wife relationship. As this has proved to be a critical juncture in our analysis, it would be wise, at this time, to cast our net more widely in hopes of finding broader social trends that would support our argument. Let us first examine evidence relating to the participation of women in activities other than familial, especially participation in the labor force.

If husband-wife role differentiation were, in fact, integrative of the marital relationship, we would expect to see this reflected in the labor force participation of wives. Specifically, we would expect to find few wives working and even fewer mothers working. In rather sharp contrast to this expectation, data from the United States Census indicate that husbands are the sole recipients of income in only 44 percent of all families where both husband and wife are present.[11] Moreover, as Farber points out, these same data indicate that the differences usually found between working and nonworking wives with regard to the numbers of children ever born (per 1,000 women) are declining.[12] That is, it appears that having children is losing force as a deterrent to the wife's seeking employment. More direct evidence of this increase in the numbers of mothers at work indicates that in the decade 1949-58, the number of mothers of children under twelve who were in the labor force rose from three million to 5.4 million, an increase of 80 percent.[13] In other words, not only does it appear that wives, in general, are increasingly seeking employment, but, even more important, the traditional barriers to continued employment, bearing and raising children, are as strong as they once were. With or without children, working wives are becoming more common. The increasing demand, in urban areas around the country, for sharply increased day-care facilities bear witness to the fact that mothers are now less content to be only mothers.[14]

Of course, many of the working wives and mothers work out of necessity, not out of choice, and, thus, it is not entirely accurate to speak as though all working wives (or even the majority, necessarily) are working so as to reduce the levels of differentiation in their marriages. Unfortunately, we know of no data that allow us to examine the extent of wives working, while simultaneously including data on age and number of children and the economic status of the family. Were such data available, we could then examine only those cases where the level of income is high enough to assume that economic need is not the primary compelling force in the wife's decision to work. The only data we have seen that are somewhat relevant to this issue deliberately exclude mothers with children under eighteen years of age. Nonetheless, the figures are worth citing as long as the reader remains aware of the caveat: no children under eighteen. The figures (1951) are as follows: "Of wives between the ages of 22 and 44 whose husbands were earning under $5,000 a year..., about 55 percent were at work. At the husband's income level between $5,000 and $7,000...30 percent of the wives went to work. In the $7,000-$10,000 bracket, only 8.6 percent of the wives were working. But of the $10,000-and-over group, 21.1 percent of the wives had taken jobs."[15] The women in the most affluent group are clearly not working out of economic need. What the trends are in this regard, and how the above figures would be altered were wives with young children also included are questions that remain unanswerable.[16]

The importance of these questions cannot be overemphasized. For if it does turn out that middle class wives are increasingly seeking satisfactions outside the confines of the differentiated feminine role of housekeeper-mother, whether these satisfactions are to be found, by some, in working or, by others, in going back to school or becoming involved in voluntary organizations, it will nevertheless be clear that what we have traced in our sample of couples is a more general phenomenon involving far larger numbers of married couples. If one were to believe the impressionistic accounts now quite current about the frustrated and bored suburban housewife, our search would be made much easier. However, we are willing to wait until more systematic data are made available. While we need not rush to accept impressionistic reports, it does seem significant for us to note, in passing, that several recent works have dealt with issues that closely parallel, and frequently overlap, those that are raised in this study. The most widely known of these has been Betty Friedan's The Feminine Mystique.[17] While much of this book relies on annecdotal materials relating the plight of the housewife who feels adrift and without purpose, there is a good deal of material from a wide range of studies, psychological and sociological, that points in the same direction as our data--viz., that role differentiation in the family carries with it strains that are manifested in husband-wife conflict and declines in marital gratification. In a similar vein, a recent article by Alice S. Rossi makes substantially the same point.[18] While neither of these works helps very much in determining how widespread the phenomena that we are discussing are, the mere fact that these issues are beginning to be raised and discussed is some indication that our data have bearing on conditions that extend beyond our sample of four hundred couples.

The implications of the above remarks are that the wife should diversify her marital roles and thereby make her life and her marriage more satisfying--to herself and her husband. Our data indicate that there is another way for couples to avoid the dilemmas of increasing differentiation and decreasing gratification. The husband can simply hold back and not get overinvolved in his occupational pursuits. Recent work in occupational sociology indicates that this may in fact be occuring within certain middle class occupations, especially those in the large corporations.[19] Frequently noted, in this regard, are the problems of middle management. At this level, the number of higher positions drops off precipitously and one of the adaptations to the strain inherent in the quest for promotion is simply to stop trying and transfer energies from the corporation to the family.[20] Again, though, it is impossible to discover how widespread this is. The fact that, according to Whyte, corporations are becoming interested in the wives of their managers, however, is evidence that this is not an uncommon problem. Apparently, the corporation is interested in seeing to it that the wife, as well as her husband, feels "a part of" the corporate "family" and by involving her, indirectly, the hope is that she will support her husband so that his commitments to the organization will not falter.[21] The corporation, in recognizing the threat of a disaffected wife, also recognizes the source of this threat--the distance that is created between husband and wife when the former commits himself to a career and the latter remains at home, an alien to the world of work and its attendant values and demands.

It is this dilemma, by no means peculiar to the corporate "organization men," that has been the single most important factor in determining the changes in the husband-wife relationship that we have observed taking place in our sample of couples. Even our very cursory glimpse at several recent broad social trends indicates that there is reason to entertain the possibility that what we have observed in microcosm represents a fundamental source of continued change in the relationship between family and occupational structure and, hence, a change in the family and/or occupational structures of our society. It is important to note, albeit in passing, that the source of such dynamic as may appear seems to be internal to the family. That is, in assessing the future changes that may occur, our analysis indicates that the family cannot be viewed simply as a passive agent, reacting to but never adding to pressures for change.

As to whether or not change will occur--and if it does, whether it occurs for some of the reasons discussed in this work--only time will tell. This truism, however, should not be mistaken for passivity: time reveals change to those who are willing to look for it. If nothing else, our analysis indicates that the search is warranted.

FOOTNOTES

1. Pineo, op. cit., p. 5.

2. William J. Goode, "Family Disorganization," in Robert K. Merton and Robert A. Nisbet (eds.), Contemporary Social Problems (New York: Harcourt, Brace and World, 1961), p. 441.

3. Blood and Wolfe, op. cit., pp. 68-72.

4. Parsons and Bales, op. cit., esp. Chapters One and Five.

5. Blood and Wolfe, as we have mentioned, present disconnected data bearing on this issue. See our discussion of this in Chapter Two.

6. Prodipto, Roy, "Maternal Employment and Adolescent Roles: Rural-Urban Differentials," in William J. Goode, (ed.), Readings on the Family and Society (Englewood Cliffs, N.J.: Prentice-Hall, Inc., 1964), pp. 144-51. Numerous other studies on this have produced mixed results, but the balance appears to weigh in the favor of no differences between children of employed mothers and mothers staying at home. For a comprehensive review of this literature, see Alberta E. Siegel and Miriam B. Haas, "The Working Mother: A Review of Research," Child Development (September, 1963), 34:3:513-42.

7. Robert R. Sears, Eleanor E. Maccoby and Harry Levin, Patterns of Child Rearing. Cited in Farber, op. cit., p. 451.

8. In the Roy study cited in footnote 6 above, urban boys (but not girls) reported higher levels of cooperation and democracy in their families when the mother was employed. We take this as a possible indication that boys see more of their fathers in families where the mother works as a result of continued sharing of socialization responsibilities. Thus boys, but not necessarily girls, feel more a part of the family process. This, of course, is only a hypothesis; no study to this author's knowledge has tested this directly.

9. We are not disputing the assertion that husband-wife role differentiation occurs. Granting its occurrence, we are questioning the assumption that this differentiation is integrative. For a critical review of the Parsons-Bales volume stressing similar doubts as to the usefulness of the empirical basis of Parsons' generalizations, see Nelson N. Foote, "Parsonian Theory of Family Process: "Family, Socialization and Interaction Process," Sociometry (1956), 19:40-46.

10. We have not entertained the possibility that husbands may throw themselves into an occupational role with increasing vigor in compensation for a lack of marital gratification. While this is logically possible and sociologically plausible, this interpretation would not, we think, account for the observed relationships between wife's working and husband-wife participation in organizations, on the one hand, and marital conflict and loss of gratification on the other.

11. Farber, op. cit., p. 127. The data Farber bases this figure on are taken from the U.S. Bureau of the Census, "Family Characteristics of Persons: March, 1959," Current Population Reports, Series P-20, No. 112, December 29, 1961.

12. Ibid., p. 129.

13. Women's Bureau, Day Care of Children Under 12, U.S. Department of Labor, Women's Bureau, 1960, p. 1.

14. A thoroughgoing analysis of the growth of day care facilities and the implications of this growth can be found in Burt Wallrich, Social Change in a Welfare Society: Growth of the Day Care Program, unpublished M.A. thesis,

Department of Sociology, University of California, Berkeley (1966), esp. pp. 124-40 and 182-216.

15. Daniel Bell, "The Great Back-to-Work Movement," Fortune (July, 1956), cited in Harold L. Wilensky and Charles N. Lebeaux, Industrial Society and Social Welfare (New York: The Free Press of Glencoe, 1965), p. 127. Data reported by Blood and Wolfe, without indicating the presence or age of children, indicate no tendency for an upturn in the employment of wives at the upper income level. Blood and Wolfe, op. cit., p. 98.

16. The impression one gets from the literature on working wives, however, is distinctly that of an increase in the frequency of employed, middle class wives, both with and without children. For example, Nye and Hoffman remark: "...A transition was made from a situation in which women were forced into employment, with their labor the primary source of family income, to one in which women are drawn into employment to raise family living standards or for other reasons." They go on to indicate that the middle class is also involved in this process. F. Ivan Nye and Lois Wladis Hoffman, The Employed Mother in America (Chicago: Rand McNally and Co., 1963), pp. 12-13.

17. (New York: W.W. Norton, 1963).

18. "Equality Between the Sexes: An Immodest Proposal," Daedalus (1964), 93:614-28.

19. For example, see Robert Rapoport and Rhonda Rapoport, "Work and Family in Contemporary Society," American Sociological Review (June, 1965), 30:381-94.

20. See Fred H. Goldner, "Demotion in Industrial Management," American Sociological Review (October, 1965), 30:723. Also, Wilensky, "Work, Careers, and Social Integration," op. cit.

21. William H. Whyte, Jr. "The Wives of Management," in Philip Olson (ed.), America as a Mass Society (New York: The Free Press of Glencoe, 1963), pp. 478-91.

APPENDIX: A DESCRIPTION OF THE INDICES OF MARITAL RELATIONSHIPS USED IN THIS WORK

Each of the following indices were developed in the course of Burgess' work on the family and have been used in this study without modification. The only index not presented here is the Marital Adjustment Score. This measure has been extensively discussed in the literature of the family. For a discussion of its nature, and of its strengths and weaknesses, see Burgess and Wallin, Engagement and Marriage. For the remaining measures--Dominance, Consensus, Traditionalism, Happiness, Love, Permanence and Idealization--both the questions making up these various indices and the scoring procedure for each are given below.

I. Dominance Score

Question	Scoring		
I have a need for someone who lets me have my own way..............	yes	2	(to self)
Do you usually try to avoid arguments?	no	2	(to self)
Do you lose your temper easily?........	yes	2	(to self)
Do you try to get your own way even if you have to fight for it?........	yes	2	(to self)
In your relations with the opposite sex, do you tend to be dominant and have your own way?..............	yes	2	(to self)

Compare on the scale that follows the personality traits of your spouse and yourself:

	Very much so....... 4
Angers easily	Considerably........ 3
Stubborn	Somewhat........... 2
Dominating	A little............. 1
	Not at all.......... 0

Score for this segment is the sum of the points of self rating plus those of the spouse's rating.

My mate is argumentative My mate is quick tempered My mate criticizes me	negative response.... 0 all others.......... 2

If you could, what things would you change in your mate and yourself?
If mentions: stubbornness, add 2
timidity, add -2

What things does your mate do that you do not like? If mentions:
tries to take the lead, add 2 to spouse
lack of self-confidence, add -2 to spouse

What things do you do that your mate does not like? If mentions:
insisting on own way, add 2 to self
lack of initiative, add -2 to self

When disagreements arise between you and your mate, do they usually result in:

	Self	Spouse
your giving in..................	-4	4
your mate's giving in...........	4	-4
agreement by mutual give and take	0	0

The score for the person is the sum of his individual ratings of himself and his spouse's ratings. Maximum score is 56. The higher the score, the more dominant the respondent.

II. Consensus

Question	Scoring
What is your attitude toward having children? What is your mate's attitude? Check whether desire children: very much; a good deal; somewhat; a little; not at all.	same.................... 5 difference of 1.......... 4 difference of 2.......... 3 difference of 3.......... 1 difference of 4.......... 0
Do you and your mate attend	the same church........ 1 different churches 0

Indicate your approximate agreement or disagreement with your spouse on the following matters:

a. handling of family finances
b. matters of recreation

c. religious matters
d. demonstration of affection
e. friends
f. table manners
g. matters of conventionality
h. philosophy of life
i. ways of dealing with your families
j. wife's working
k. intimate relations
l. sharing household tasks
m. politics

Model:	
always agree	5
almost always agree	4
occasionally disagree	3
frequently disagree	2
almost always disagree	1
always disagree	0

How many serious quarrels have you had with your spouse in the past 12 months?

Scoring	
4 or more	0
3	1
2	2
1	3
0	4

Maximum score is 85. The higher the score, the greater the agreement between spouses as perceived by the respondent.

III. Happiness

Question	Scoring (from 13, add or subtract as indicated)
Place a check before any of the following statements which represent your feelings about your marriage or your spouse:	
Although my mate and I get along well together, I think I could be happier married to someone else	-1
I believe our marriage is reasonably happy	-1
My marriage is a very happy one	1
I don't think anyone could possibly be happier with one another	1
I have never thought of my marriage as having made me particularly happy or not	-1
Although I am usually happy with my spouse, he (she) occasionally makes me feel miserable	-1
My marriage is happier than average but less so than the very successful ones	-1
My marriage borders on being unhappy	-1
I think I could be much happier if I had married someone else	-1

My marriage could be much happier than it is	-1
My marriage is a happy one	1
I think my marriage is neither more nor less happy than most	-1
I can't conceive of anyone being more happily married than I am	1
I'm quite happily married	-1
My marriage is an unhappy one	-1
I've known very little happiness in my marriage	-1

Question	Scoring	
If until now your marriage has been at all unhappy, how confident are you that it will work out all right in the future?	very confident	3
	confident	2
	somewhat uncertain	1
	has not been at all unhappy	4
Everything considered, how happy has your marriage been for you?	extraordinarily happy	8
	decidedly happy	7
	happy	6
	somewhat happy	5
	average	4
	somewhat unhappy	3
	unhappy	2
	decidedly unhappy	1
	extremely unhappy	0
If your marriage is now at all unhappy, how long has it been so: _______ months.	blank	3
	less than 3 months	2
	3-11 months	1
	12 or more months	0
Even if satisfied with your spouse, have you ever felt that you might have been at all happier married to another type of man (woman)?	frequently	0
	occasionally	1
	rarely	2
	never	3

Maximum score is 32. The higher the score, the greater the happiness.

IV. Permanence

Question	Scoring	
Have you ever considered departing from your mate?	seriously	0
	somewhat seriously	1
	not seriously	2
	have never considered	3

Question	Scoring
If you have never considered separation or divorce, has this been because of (check): religious principles; wouldn't be fair to spouse; not liking to admit failure; the effect it would have on your children; what people would think of you; couldn't do better in another marriage; never remarry; the effect on business or career; other.	none checked.......... 1 1 or more checked 0
If you have never considered separation or divorce, is it because you are satisfied with spouse?	yes.......... 1 no 0
Have you ever considered divorcing your spouse?	seriously......... 0 somewhat seriously 1 not seriously ..... 2 never considered.. 3

Maximum score is 8. The higher the score, the less consideration of divorce and/or separation.

MARITAL SUCCESS SCORE INDEX

Love score

Question		Scoring	
Own love--Indicate to what extent you are in love with your mate by placing a check in one square on the boxed line below which ranges from "extraordinarily in love" to "somewhat in love." If your feelings fluctuate between two points, indicate what they are by placing a check in each of the boxes (A-J).	extraordinarily	A....9 B....8 C....7 D....6 E....5 F....4 G....3 H....2 I....1	(2 or more checks, take lower score.)
	somewhat	J....0	
Has your mate ever doubted your love for her (him)?		never........... 4 once............ 3 rarely.......... 2 occasionally..... 1 often 0	

IDEALIZATION SCORE INDEX

Questions	Scoring (rating of mate)
Compare on the scale which follows the personality traits of your husband and yourself.	
Angers easily	very much so..... 0
Stubborn	considerably...... 1
Selfish	somewhat......... 2
Irritable	a little........... 3
Moody	not at all......... 4
Net score is EX_i / N.	

TRADITIONALISM SCORE INDEX

Question	Scoring
How important is it for the ideal marriage that:	
(a) the husband should wear the pants	very necessary for happy marriage.............. 5 usually desirable....... 4 makes little or no difference .... 3 usually not desirable.... 2 decidedly not desirable .. 1
(b) the wife should have money of her own	decidedly not desirable .. 5 usually not desirable.... 4 makes little or no difference................. 3 usually desirable .... 2 very necessary for happy marriage.............. 1
(c) children should be held to strict discipline	same as (a)
(d) husband and wife should not have had sexual intercourse with each other before marriage	same as (a)
(e) young people should be	

trained never to indulge in "petting" or "spooning"	same as (a)

Score is the sum of score X number of questions divided by the number of questions answered.